THE ART OF
WRITING
BUSINESS
REPORTS &
PROPOSALS

THE ART OF
WRITING
BUSINESS
REPORTS &
PROPOSALS

BY

HOWARD HILLMAN

COAUTHOR: LISA LORING

ILLUSTRATED BY PATRICIA E. NEAL

THE VANGUARD PRESS, NEW YORK

Designer: Tom Bevans
Manufactured in the United States of America
1 2 3 4 5 6 7 8 9 0
Library of Congress Cataloging in Publication Data
Hillman, Howard.
The art of writing business reports & proposals.
Bibliography: p.
1.   Business report writing.   2.   Proposal writing
in business.   I.   Title.   II.   Title: Business reports
& proposals.
HF5719.H54   808'.066651021   81-3316
ISBN 0-8149-0850-0   AACR2

CONTENTS

PREFACE

Career advancement depends, to a large measure, on the ability to write effective business reports and proposals. My book will give you a competitive edge by helping you acquire this profitable expertise.

The art of writing business reports and proposals can be one of the handiest tools in your executive-skill box. Reports are the tried and true means for communicating and recording vital information that is the basis for making intelligent business decisions. The written proposal is usually your most effective instrument for convincing a prospective client to sign on the dotted line or for persuading your boss to approve your pet project. Yet few people take the time and make the effort to learn how to use proficiently that report- and proposal-writing tool.

You are often judged more by your written than by your spoken words. In today's increasingly complex and geographically dispersed business world, for example, your contact with your boss's boss (the person who has much to say about your future promotions and salary hikes) may consist mainly of written rather than face-to-face encounters. Not only will your reports or proposals influence how he or she views your mastery of the subject at hand, they will also help shape his or her evaluation of how clearly you are able to think in general. Depending on how well you have developed your ability to write those documents (and it is largely an acquired skill), the preparation of reports and proposals can be an opportunity or pitfall for your career.

An ill-written report or proposal does more than kill opportunity and reputation — it wastes company resources. The dollar value of the writer's and secretary's time for the preparation of a simple one-page memo report or proposal, according to a recent estimate, averages $19.34. Add the cost of the reader's time, and the expenditure increases. If the document spans a score or more pages, the outlay can run into hundreds if not thousands of dollars. Calculate the number of reports and proposals that are prepared each year within a department or company, and the total number of disbursed dollars can be staggering. Any firm that spends money to teach its employees how to write productive reports and proposals is making an investment that will pay hefty dividends in the future.

The Art of Writing Business Reports and Proposals is not an academic textbook designed to expound theory. Rather, my book is written for the experienced business person who needs and wants gutsy field-tested tips and insights, the ones that reap profits in real life. While my book cannot guarantee you financial success, it certainly will increase the odds in your favor.

— Howard Hillman

PART ONE

Report Writing

Introduction to Part One

Written reports are vital in today's complex business world. Without them, information — the lifeblood of decision-making — would flow sluggishly through the corporate veins, debilitating the organism.

The larger the organization, the more business reports are necessary. In Goliathan corporations, for instance, coordination through reports is a must, since job responsibilities tend to be specialized and isolated, yet each person's role within those firms is crucially interrelated with many other posts.

The speed at which scientific breakthroughs, policy shifts, personnel turnover, and other vicissitudes occur within the business sphere also makes reports indispensable. Without a steady stream of those documents, a person couldn't possibly keep up to date with all the latest developments within his or her field.

The variety of reports used in business is boundless. Here's but a brief sampling:

annual report ✓
auditor's report ✓
claims report ✓
conference report ✓
credit report ✓
laboratory report ✓
minutes of a meeting ✓
market survey report ✓

personnel evaluation report
plant-inspection report
product evaluation report
profit-and-loss statement
progress report
sales-call report
seminar agenda
stockholders' report
tax report

While there are some similarities between a report and a proposal, a fundamental distinction exists, as is made clear by this tautology: a report reports and a proposal proposes. In a report your self-interests are irrelevant. The implicit mission of a report is to present facts and opinions (if germane, authoritative, and solicited) on a specific subject so that readers can keep abreast and can make rational decisions.

The easiest way to prepare a report is to approach the task systematically by breaking it down into three sequential phases: pre-writing, writing, and post-writing. Each phase is discussed in its own chapter.

Pre-Writing Phase

Some reports resemble the horns on a steer: a point here, a point there, and a ton of bull in between. The best way to avoid having a report described in those disparaging terms is to do the necessary research before starting to write the first draft. This includes trying to determine who the readers are and what they require and desire from your report.

DETERMINE WHO WILL READ YOUR REPORT

By this directive we mean more than knowing the names, titles, and job responsibilities of your readers. You must delve much deeper. What is their demographic makeup? Do the readers have similar or disparate backgrounds? Does the subject matter of the report affect them equally? How familiar are they with you and the subject matter?

You must also attempt to learn something about their business personalities and traits. For instance, do they have any biases or blind spots concerning you and the subject matter? Are they hard-nosed prove-it-to-me types?

DETERMINE WHAT IS EXPECTED OF YOU

If you are going to spend hours, days, or weeks preparing a report, invest at least a few minutes asking the persons who requested the document for an unequivocal definition of its objective, scope, limitations, and deadlines. Also query them on how they plan to use the information. Don't guess or your report may end up talking around the subject or going off on a tangent, much to the displeasure of your readers.

The prudent report writer gets his or her assignment in writing. Oral explanations tend to be ambiguous and are subject to future misinterpretations.

If you cannot obtain the request in writing, scribe it yourself and submit it for approval or simply keep it as a matter of record for your own protection. We know of one executive who nearly had the career rug pulled from under her feet because she didn't prepare the type of report that her boss claimed he had assigned to her. Fortunately, she had a copy of a memo that she sent to him reiterating his oral instructions. She got off the hook because if she were off-target, the boss should have corrected her aim when he received her recapitulation.

DETERMINE THE NATURE OF YOUR REPORT

Virtually all the reports you write can be grouped into one of the following classifications:

Data-giving Reports

Analysis-giving Reports

Advice-giving Reports

The distinctions among these three categories must be understood by anyone who has been assigned a report.

A data-giving report presents relevant facts and authoritative opinions (but never your personal opinions) in a clear, logical sequence. When appropriate, it also describes your research sources and methodology. A data-giving report leaves the work of drawing conclusions and formulating courses of action exclusively to the readers. For instance, you may be asked to research and report "the employee turnover rates and the salary levels at our plants in Miami, Albuquerque, and Seattle."

The analysis-giving report is a fact-giving report with one additional feature: you are asked to interpret the data you present. Thus, in the example in the preceding paragraph, you may be asked to evaluate whether there is any meaningful correlation between the employee-turnover rates and the salary levels at the three plants.

The advice-giving report adds yet another element: your counsel. After presenting and interpreting the data, you are expected to suggest to the readers what should and should not be done. If, for instance, your evaluation indicated that there was a legitimate and significant relationship between the turnover rates and salaries, you would recommend one or more appropriate courses of action.

DETERMINE WHICH GOES FIRST:
THE EVIDENCE OR THE CONCLUSIONS

Try to determine whether your readers prefer that you state your interpretations and recommendations up front — that is, in the introduction of your report. Most readers want you to do so; they do not want a report to read like a suspense thriller. Whereas they would be piqued at the mystery writer who revealed that "the butler did it" in the book's opening paragraph, they would be just as mad at the report writer who made them wade through the entire document in order to discover its conclusions.

There are times, however, when it is good psychology to hold back the report's interpretations and recommendations until you have prepared the readers for them. Examples of such instances are when the news is negative or runs counter to the readers' beliefs or expectations; when the readers bear hostility to you or the subject matter; when the conclusions are new and unorthodox; when the readers prefer to work their way through the evidence before reading the conclusions.

DETERMINE THE BEST MEDIUM

Before penning your first word, you must decide which medium best suits your report. Your basic options are:

> Formal Report
> Informal Report:
>> Letter Report
>> Memo Report
>> Form Report

No one medium is the ideal choice for all business situations and some companies have set policies on when to use each medium. Should your client or firm not have engraved rules, here are some practical guidelines:

A formal report is the one you should usually choose when your communication is lengthy or deals with a subject of considerable consequence. By its very nature, a formal report draws attention to the significance of your data. This medium also enables you — when appropriate — to embellish your document with a touch of grandness. (We discuss the intricacies of designing the format of a formal report in the next chapter, Writing Phase, starting on page 19.)

While both the letter and memo reports are classified as informal reports, the letter is considered more formal than the memo. Consequently, most corporations follow this guideline: use a letter for informal reports that go outside the company and a memo for those that stay within the firm.

A form report is a handy device when the information is routine, as it is in an expense, income-tax, or customer-call report. When you design a form, you make it easier for the respondent to complete the report. All he or she needs to do is to check off answers or fill in the blank spaces. A form report benefits you too. You determine what data flows to you. And you receive that input in one uniform and therefore easy-to-compile format. You are thus in a good position to cross-analyze information from various respondents and periods.

DETERMINE THE MOST APPROPRIATE WRITING STYLE

Another pre-writing decision that you must make involves selecting the most fitting writing style for your report. A medley of factors should influence your choice. Above all, stick with a style that is natural to you. By writing in a mode in which you feel comfortable and confident, you save time and energy. Even more important, because using your own style allows you to express your ideas more clearly, you stand a better chance of getting your message across to the readers.

When we suggest that you write in your own style, we

do not mean that you should do so in a vacuum. You must adapt your style to the needs of your reader and subject matter. Some fields, such as investment banking, tend to have tacit rules that reports be written in a conservative tone while others, such as the entertainment industry, often respond to creative flair. The trick is to make some accommodation, but not to an extent that corrupts the integrity of your natural style.

The terms "formal" and "informal" are not clear-cut when applied to business-writing style. What one executive considers a formal tone may seem informal to another. When writing in a formal style, some prefer to use the third rather than the first person because, they argue, it conveys objectivity. Thus they would write, "It is recommended" rather than, "I recommend." We believe that writers should not be afraid to pen "I" or "we" when they are stating their own opinions because a first-person pronoun gives the text more vitality than does a third-person "it."

Too many report writers — especially those with a bureaucratic bent — purposely use the pedantic and stilted style normally associated with scientific papers. They mistakenly believe that it will make their reports seem more authoritative. What gives a scientific paper its authority is its author's knowledge. It just so happens that most authors of scientific papers are horrendous writers. If they were able to write in a less stuffy style, their learned discussions would be clearer and therefore carry even greater authority.

Customarily, the tone of a formal report tends to be slightly more reserved than that of a memo, letter, or form report. That rule of thumb, however, should not be followed blindly. If, for instance, you are writing a formal report to a client with whom you are on amiable terms, its tone would probably be more relaxed than that of a memo report designed for one of your firm's executive vice presidents with whom you have had scant contact.

Whatever your style, be sure it does not get in the way of clear communication. You probably have come across a report written by a person who viewed it as a showcase for his or her undiscovered literary talents rather than as a means to convey information. A document of this breed reveals more about the writer than it does about the subject matter.

DETERMINE THE IDEAL LENGTH

Another of your research goals is to determine the ideal length for your report. That length should be a function of several variables. Tops on the list are the complexity of the subject, the readers' grasp of that subject, and the amount of documentation that the subject and readers require. A reader's interest in the report and his or her available time to review the document are also considerations, as is the amount of time that you can realistically allocate to its preparation.

What some report writers lack in depth, they try to compensate for in length. When all is said and done, they just keep on writing. As a general rule of thumb, the shorter the report, the greater the chances it will be read carefully (if at all) and therefore the greater the chances that the reader will absorb its contents. However, it would be arbitrary to set a maximum — or, for that matter, a minimum — length. We have seen reports varying from three words to, at the other extreme, over a million words spread over five thousand pages bound into a back-breaking ten-volume set. Each was suited to and accomplished its purpose. The first was the terse message that Julius Caesar sent back to the Roman Senate to announce his victory in Asia Minor: "*Veni, vidi, vici*" ("I came, I saw, I conquered"). The second was a report from a government contractor to the U.S. Army. (No, we didn't have to read it.)

Memo and letter reports are typically one page or less and seldom more than several pages.

QUESTION THE REPORT'S COST-EFFECTIVENESS

Report writing is a far more expensive process than most executives realize. If they kept a detailed time log of every hour that goes into the preparation of their reports, they might be astonished.

One of the best ways to cut down on report-writing expenditures is to reduce the number of reports you and your staff prepare. Get in the habit of asking, "Is this report vital?" and "Will its value justify its cost?"

CONSTRUCT A PRELIMINARY FORMAT

Once you have clearly understood the report's purpose, scope, and limitations, draft a preliminary outline of its format. This skeletal model will require modifications as you proceed, but it is imperative that you have some blueprint to guide you in the development of your research plan.

(Note: you wil find a detailed discussion on report formats in the next chapter, "Writing Phase".)

DEVISE A RESEARCH PLAN OF ACTION

A good research plan saves much time and money. Besides helping to keep you pointed in the right direction, a research plan helps keep you on target as to deadlines and budgeted work-hours. This last function — work-hours — can prohibitively escalate the cost of research if not held in tight rein. When one gets involved in researching an interesting topic, there is a tendency to lose track of time. A good researcher recognizes that time is money and that there is a point of diminishing returns for the hours spent digging up data. At the same time, keep in mind that under-researching is just as costly. If you base your analysis on incomplete data, your conclusions and recommendations are bound to be faulty unless you make a very lucky guess. Always bear in mind: the difference between guessing and knowing is having sufficient evidence at hand.

Indicate in your research plan all the critical data that you believe has to be collected. Specify how, where, when, and by whom it will be gathered.

AVOID NEEDLESS RESEARCH

Investigate whether the required data is already available elsewhere. Since the amount of money spent on unnecessary firsthand research can be stunning, it pays to scan sources such as trade publications, your company files, and the public library. Your colleagues, too, can be founts of ready-to-use information.

Expenditures can also be pruned by relating your report to those previously published. You can excerpt relevant portions or, if you are sure the other documents are readily available to your readers, you can simply refer them to the right place.

KEEP YOUR GOAL IN MIND

As you research, keep asking yourself, "What do my readers need and want?" It is easy to lose track of the forest for the trees by concentrating on interesting though tangential or uncrucial details.

RESEARCH WITH AN OBJECTIVE EYE

A number of report writers fit H.L. Mencken's definition of a cynic: "A man who, when he smells flowers, looks around for a coffin." These are the writers who, for instance, mistakenly believe that a serious problem exists simply because they were asked to do a report. While doing their research, they view their microcosm through gray-colored eyeglasses, which is as much of a transgression as viewing it through rose-colored ones. Or the writers blindly accept their own or the reader's untested assumptions and pooh-pooh contradictory evidence. There is nothing wrong with

— and much good to be said for — informing the readers that the problem is different than or not as severe as they had originally believed, if that be the case.

REASON RATIONALLY

This book is not a primer on the art of reasoning. Books galore have been written on that subject. We can, however, point out a few of the failings in thinking that reoccur in day-to-day report writing.

Don't confuse instinct with reality. Instinct is, to paraphrase Oscar Wilde, that strange feeling that convinces people they are right when they are not.

Don't necessarily accept a popular opinion as fact because it may be a misconception that has obtained homage with age. Also keep in mind that time or events may have transformed a former fact into fiction. Get on solid ground with a quick telephone call to an informed individual. Better to appear ignorant to that one person than to your readers at large.

Don't jump to conclusions. Be sure you have gathered and analyzed all the pertinent data before you send your "open-and-shut" case to the jury — your readers.

Recognize the difference between deductive and inductive reasoning. In deductive reasoning, the conclusion is absolute and irrefutable. An example is: "All Rainbow Widget distributors make money. The Sphinx Company is a Rainbow Widget distributor. Therefore, the Sphinx Company makes money." With inductive reasoning, there is insufficient evidence to draw a conclusion that is valid beyond a shadow of a doubt. For instance: "All Rainbow Widget distributors make money. Therefore, if we become a Rainbow Widget distributor, we will make money."

Inductive reasoning can be sound or not. Assume that in front of you are one hundred boxes labeled "marbles." If you randomly open fifty and discover that their contents consists exclusively of yellow marbles, you will not be violating the rules of rational thinking if you say, "Chances are the next box I open will contain yellow marbles." On the other hand, people will rightfully think that you've lost your marbles should you draw the same conclusion after opening only two of the one hundred boxes.

Don't use selective evidence that unfairly substantiates a preconceived conclusion. If, for instance, you have polled one hundred customers and sixty of them gave answers that supported your hypothesis, avoid the temptation of merely saying, "Sixty customers I polled agreed that . . ." without tagging on "while forty . . .".

SELECT THE MOST EFFICIENT INTERVIEWING MEDIUM

When you must solicit facts and opinions from individuals, select the most efficient medium for your particular set of circumstances.

The quickest source is that plastic contraption that sits on your desk within a convenient arm's reach. However, the telephone is generally not effective if the number of questions or interviewees is many or if you are an unknown quantity to the person on the receiver end. The latter situation is an especially significant factor when the interviewee fears that his or her answers may beget negative repercussions.

Face-to-face interviews eat up more time and increase the risk that the interviewer's positive or negative bearing will influence the responses. On the other hand, face-to-face encounters generally enable the interviewer to ask questions of a more personal or controversial nature. They also allow the interviewer to observe nonverbal language and, therefore, to better interpret the answers and to adjust the line of questioning when necessary.

Before you walk into an interview have your questions and strategy down pat and, if necessary, rehearsed. Once in the meeting, listen carefully. This advice may seem obvious, but recent research studies by a responsible survey group show that the average executive listens at a 25 percent level of efficiency — and that the ideas and data communicated in a meeting can be distorted by as much as 80 percent as they progress through the organization. Poor listening is a common and costly habit.

A questionnaire is usually your best bet when interviewees are numerous or geographically distant. It is also worth employing when the questions exceed a handful, when they require more than an off-the-cuff answer, or when anonymity is necessary. A questionnaire is also a handy tool when you want to make a quick and easy comparison of the various answers to any given question.

To be effective, a questionnaire must be clear, inviting, and easy to answer. Get the interviewee's pen moving by starting off with questions that can be readily answered. Save the more thought-provoking questions for later when the respondent is into the groove.

The longer the questionnaire, the greater the likelihood that it will be tossed into the circular file. To counter indifference, be sure to highlight in a headline or in a cover letter the significance of the answers as they relate to the respondent. To encourage high response rate, offer to share the survey results with the respondent and enclose a stamped, self-addressed, return envelope.

Yet another tactic for increasing questionnaire response is to ask a question or two bordering on the controversial. Studies have shown that when people are given an opportunity to vent their steam and to stand up and be counted, the percentage of returned questionnaires increases appreciably.

Writing Phase

Mary Heaton Vorse wryly noted that writing is "the art of applying the seat of the pants to the seat of the chair." You will discover that you have to spend less time glued to your seat if, before you start writing your report, you design the ideal format for presenting your gathered material. By format, we mean the sequence in which you present your information.

SELECT THE BEST FORMAT

In order to select the best format for any given report you must be familiar with the fundamental components of the formal report. Once you have that knowledge under your belt, you should find it easy to design a format for an informal report — be it letter, memo, or form. After all, an informal report is in effect a pruned version of a formal report.

The next thirteen sections, therefore, concentrate on the formal report. Then we give tips and insights that relate specifically to informal letter, memo, and form reports.

PICTURE THE FORMAL REPORT IN PERSPECTIVE

A formal report in its full glory has four fundamental parts:

> Cover letter
>
> Front matter
>
> Text proper
>
> Back matter

The front matter comprises four components:

> Title page
>
> Contents
>
> Letter of Authorization
>
> Abstract

The text proper (the heart of your report) consists of three components:

> Introduction
>
> Body
>
> Conclusions

The back matter contains three components:

> Appendix
>
> Bibliography
>
> Index

No doubt some of your formal reports will not contain all ten components. A letter of authorization, for instance, is not always existent or pertinent.

We examine the cover letter and the ten components individually in ensuing sections. For a sample formal report containing title page, introduction, body, and conclusions, see page 189.

WRITE THE COVER LETTER

The time to compose your cover letter is, of course, after you have drafted all ten components of your report. We discuss it here, however, because it is the opening salvo of your report from the reader's point of view.

A well-written cover letter (also called letter of transmittal) tells the readers what you would tell them if you planned to deliver the report in person. Its primary purpose is to orient readers in the event that they are unaware of or have forgotten your document's purpose and significance.

Your cover letter should be brief and straightforward. Lead off with an opening sentence that states in so many words: "Here's the report . . .". Promptly state its title, objective, and impact. Relate the report to the readers (". . . that you requested" or ". . . that shows how to reduce your operating costs"). Define the report's scope and, if applicable, its limitations (". . . based on studies in two of our six factories").

If you like, you may include a brief summary of your report's conclusions and recommendations. But if the report itself has an "Abstract," or an "Introduction" that contains a synopsis, you need not repeat it here.

You can use the cover letter as an opportunity to thank those people who supplied material or helped you prepare the report. Say something such as, "I am indebted to . . .".

Close your cover letter on a cordial note. If the report was assigned, for instance, you may want to thank the readers for giving you the opportunity to prepare it. Likewise, let them know you have an ongoing interest in the report, perhaps by offering to supply additional information if requested or asking to be kept informed of developments.

By adding warmth and a personal touch to your cover letter, you put the readers in a receptive frame of mind. Even if your report is written in the third person, you should liberally stud your cover letter with the pronouns "you" and

"I" (or "we"). Your personality and — if the report is going to another company — your firm's personality should come through.

Your cover letter is a letter, so use the same type of format you use for your regular letters. In virtually all cases the date and signatory on the cover letter should match those on the report's title page. The cover letter is usually not attached to the report itself. However, if you are concerned that it may be misplaced before it accomplishes its mission, clip it to or insert it inside your report.

SAMPLE COVER LETTER

Dear Christopher:

Here's the report, "Estimated Setup Costs for the New Little Rock Store," which you requested on June 17.

The estimates cover expenses up to opening day. As you suggested, I did not include inventory costs.

I owe my thanks to our personnel director, Phyllis Meyer, for estimating salary and wage costs and to our office manager, James Peters, for calculating the lease and furnishings expenses. They did a great job.

Thank you for assigning me this report. Please let me know if you need any additional data.

Best regards,

WRITE THE TITLE PAGE

Every formal report should have a title page, one that breathes with enough white space to give the document an inviting air. Since the title page is normally one of the first components of the report that readers see, and since first impressions tend to be profoundly persuasive, the import of that simple sheet of paper cannot be overemphasized.

One of the best title-page designs is the one displayed in "Sample A: Formal Report" on page 189. We and countless other report writers have used it successfully in the past.

Your title page has four parts: title, submittee, date, and submitter. The last three are easy to compose. The first, however, can cause as much tribulation as any other group of words in your entire proposal.

The title should delineate the scope of your report. Compare this title:

Profits
For Fast Food Outlets
in Nevada

and this title:

1980 Profits
For Fast Food Outlets

with this title:

1980 Profits
For Fast Food Outlets
in Nevada

The first two titles would not be specific enough to attract readers whose interests cover more than the state of Nevada or the year 1980.

A well-chosen title is particularly important if the report is to be filed for future use. The words of the title will help the filing clerk correctly pigeonhole the document and, when necessary, retrieve it. A mislabeled report not only can be overlooked; it can be pulled out when not relevant, thus wasting the time of both clerk and readers.

Stingily use words. As you pen the title, bear in mind this Madison Avenue precept: with each additional word you add to a title, you proportionately decrease the chances of its being read. A six-word title is approximately 15 percent less likely to be read than a five-word one. Up the word count to ten and the estimate escalates to about 50 percent. No better case has ever been leveled against verbiage. Ideally, the title should be one complete or fragmentary sentence. If you need a longer title, write a short title followed by a subtitle.

Generally, the date of submission should be the one that goes on the title page. An exception to the rule would be, for instance, in a report on pork-belly futures written on Friday afternoon when you are concerned that prices might change by the time you hand the report over to your boss at 9:45 Monday morning.

WRITE THE CONTENTS

If your report is lengthy, be sure to prepare a Contents. It serves as a road map, enabling the readers to locate quickly those aspects of your report that will interest them the most.

Title this component "Contents," not "Table of Contents," because the latter phrase is dated. Constructing the Contents should be a snap because it is essentially an edited version of your working outline. In fact, the items in your Contents should be identical in wording to the headings in your report, though you need not list every heading in your Contents.

If your report has a number of graphic aids and you believe that listing them in a separate table will benefit your readers, go ahead and create one. Give it a short, descriptive title ("Illustrations" or "Charts," for example).

INSERT THE LETTER OF AUTHORIZATION

A letter of authorization is written by the person who requested the report. It verifies that that person instructed the writer to prepare the report and, sometimes, it sets forth the conditions.

There are times when placing the letter of authorization (or a copy of it) in your report is advisable, if not compulsory. A case in point is a reminder to a habitually forgetful executive that he or she wrote, "Spend as much of the company's time and money as you need to in order to get me the facts — even if it means taking two trips to Tahiti." A letter of authorization ("We agree to pay your firm $23,500 to prepare this report") can also serve the function of a purchase order.

WRITE THE ABSTRACT

An abstract — which can also be called a brief, précis, or synopsis — is an indispensable component for any

— 25 —

lengthy report. It condenses the highlights for busy readers and allows them to see whether they want to read further. If they do, they can dive into part or all of the text proper.

Your abstract should touch all key bases: the purpose of your report and its most salient findings, conclusions, and recommendations. Since you must condense, you are allowed a little latitude in making generalizations, but your readers must be able to grasp fully your message and logic without having to refer to the text proper.

Present your abstract on a separate page (or pages) and restrict its length. In most cases, it should be no longer than five hundred words or 5 percent of the total words in your report, whichever is less.

By its nature, your abstract will be terser and not as literate as your whole document. However, it should be written in a style similar to that of your report. If you wrote your report in the third person, for example, do likewise in the abstract.

Draft your abstract after you have completed the text proper. One tip for making this chore easier is to use your Contents as your outline. Just fill in the flesh.

An abstract can save you printing and delivery costs. If you are in doubt as to whether certain executives will want to see your full report, send them your abstract along with a note that you will be pleased to supply them with the full report if requested. This technique allows you to broaden your audience.

WRITE THE TEXT PROPER

As mentioned earlier, the text proper of a formal report comprises three components. It also has nine subcomponents. Here is the format:

> INTRODUCTION
> BODY
>> The Problem
>> The Purpose of the Report
>> Scope and Limitations
>> Definition of Terms
>> Methodology and Sources
>> Findings
> CONCLUSIONS
>> Analysis
>> Recommendations

WRITE THE INTRODUCTION (OR INTRODUCTION AND SUMMARY)

Please note that we are discussing the "Introduction" before the "Body" and "Conclusions" subcomponents because this is its correct location in terms of format. Notwithstanding, write your "Introduction" only after you have drafted the other two components of your text proper. Otherwise your "Introduction" may not be what it should be: a sharp and accurate distillation of those two other components.

Your "Introduction" presents the highlights of the

"Body" and — to readers who want to know up front the gist of your analysis and recommendations — the highlights of your Conclusions as well. In the latter case, title this component "Introduction and Summary."

The "Introduction" fulfills several missions: it helps the readers to grasp and appreciate the problem; it gives them an overview of your report; it helps them determine whether further study of your report would be of value to them.

Brevity is a must. Your "Introduction" should be no longer than 10 percent of the combined length of the "Body" and "Conclusions." Don't dot "i's" here — that sort of detail belongs in the "Body" and "Conclusions." All you want to accomplish in your "Introduction" is to acquaint your readers with the most significant facts and opinions that you have assembled and, if called for, the pith of your interpretations and counsel.

The format of your "Introduction" should parallel the format you use in the "Body" and "Conclusions." Thus, if you adopt the format on page 27 for the "Body," you would work your way through the problem, purpose, scope and limitations, definition of terms, methodology, sources, and findings, in that order.

Granted, you could lead off with the findings and conclusions before you encapsulate the problem and other subcomponents. Report writers choose this method when they are afraid that their key findings and conclusions might be buried and lost under the other subcomponents. While this approach is effective for some non-formal reports, it should be used infrequently for formal reports because, among other reasons, it runs counter to the practical rule that a formal report should develop in a logical sequence. Anyway, if the material that precedes the findings and conclusions in your "Introduction" is pertinent and succinct, as it should be, you shouldn't be overly concerned that you will inter your findings and conclusions.

While you should always present your major findings in your "Introduction," there are times when you don't want to divulge even one iota of your conclusions at this stage. This is the case when you would gain a psychological advantage by withholding your analysis and recommendations until after the readers have waded through the complete findings contained in the "Body" of your report. (See "Determine Which Goes First: the Evidence or the Conclusions" on page 7.)

WRITE THE BODY

The essential difference between the "Introduction" and the "Body" and "Conclusions" is that the first component gives the broad brush strokes of your handiwork while the last two are your finished masterpiece, complete with all the fine details necessary to complete the picture. Nothing in the body should be left to doubt or conjecture.

No one would likely find fault with you if, in your "Introduction," you said something on the order of "The problem surfaced three years ago in the Syracuse plant." In the "Body," you must expound on that statement by giving particulars such as the location within the plant where the problem was first noticed. Chances are that in your "Introduction" you could also offer with impunity an unspecific statement such as, "I researched all the recent issues of the major science magazines." In the "Body," you must cite

— 29 —

publication titles and dates (or refer your readers to entries in your appendix or bibliography).

Open the "Body" (as well as your "Introduction") with a clear, bold statement of the problem that your report addresses, such as "Equipment failure is reducing productivity 20 percent." This tactic grabs the attention of those people who have a vested interest in the problem. What you should avoid is allowing your enthusiasm to magnify the problem out of proportion. Let the facts speak for themselves.

Defining the problem is sometimes not enough. If your readers do not have a perspective on the problem, you may also have to provide some historical background.

Not all reports, obviously, address problems. An example is a report that itemizes inventory. In such a case, you skip the statement of the problem and start off the "Body" (as well as your "Introduction") with "the purpose of the report" subcomponent, where you explain why you have prepared the report. Use direct wording such as "My purpose is to . . ." because it gets the point across quickly and surely to busy executives.

When describing your purpose, tell the readers if your report covers more than one subject. Also tell them who initiated the report.

Next, define the scope and limitations of your report. By limitations we mean both the assigned and unforeseen ones. If you couldn't gather all the facts that you required, mention it — but also explain why (an insufficient budget or an uncooperative source, for instance). This defense is necessary in order to prevent the readers from condemning you for not digging deeply or broadly enough.

Now define key words, phrases, and processes that may

be unfamiliar to your readers. Or, if you have a glossary, refer your readers to that part of your report.

Explain your research methodology, the procedures you used to gather your evidence. Be sure you demonstrate that you have used the best methodology within the limits of your available resources. Next, name your key sources. The more authoritative the sources, the more credibility you build into your report.

This brings us to the findings, the preeminent subcomponent of the "Body." Do not necessarily present all your gathered data. Use only the facts and opinions that unequivocally suit the stated purpose of your report. To illustrate what you should not include in your report, consider this hypothetical situation: You are asked to write a report on how to reduce the purchase costs of new desks. In the course of your research, you find out that there is a desk Model B that is identical to but less expensive than Model A (the one your company is currently buying). You also learn about a Model C that has the same price tag as Model A but happens to have the design that your boss avidly seeks but has never found. You would mention Model B but not Model C in your assigned report (and would herald your discovery of Model C in a separate report or in person).

How you organize your findings (and analysis and recommendations) will have a great bearing on how well you get your message across to the readers. If your findings are varied and complex, divide them into logical categories to make it easier for the readers to evaluate them.

You can organize the findings chronologically. For instance:

> First Quarter
> Second Quarter

Third Quarter

Fourth Quarter

Or you can do it on the basis of geographical location:

Northeast

Northwest

Southeast

Southwest

Or by quality:

Quality A

Quality B

Quality C

Or by quantity:

Over $1,000,000

$500,000 to $1,000,000

Under $500,000

Or by priority:

Key Customers

Major Customers

Former Customers

Or by jurisdiction:

Department A

Department B

Department C

You must, however, do more than place the collected facts and opinions in an easy-to-grasp format. You must marshall your evidence the way a trial lawyer does. Build your case by exhibiting each piece of evidence in its proper time and place. If you have done this correctly, your conclusions (or those of the readers, if your report is simply fact-finding) should be a natural outgrowth of the presented data.

At times, circumstances will dictate that you reveal

your conclusions within the fabric of the "Body" rather than in a separate component after the "Body." For instance, assume that you are asked to recommend the best type of frozen fish to import, the best mode of transportation for transferring the fish from the docks to your warehouses, and the best brand name for the product. You wouldn't wait until the end of your report to present your conclusions as to what type of fish to import because they would be too far removed from the findings on that issue. When you are faced with this kind of situation, it is wise to give your conclusions after presenting the findings for each of the major issues that your report addresses. However, because conclusions woven into the "Body" are less visible than when stated separately, you should summarize them in your "Introduction" or in a component such as "Summary of Conclusions" that would follow the "Body."

If the "Body" is just a page or so in length, give it a simple heading such as "The Report." If the "Body" is much longer, break it up with a series of headings. You could, for instance, use the subcomponents as headings ("The Problem," "The Purpose of the Report," and so forth).

WRITE THE CONCLUSIONS

In the business world, the content of this component is usually limited to the analysis and recommendations.

There are many ways to label this part of your report. You can head the whole component with a descriptive title such as "Conclusions" or "Analysis and Recommendations." If you present this component as two distinct units with one containing your interpretations and the other your counsel, then head the two units "Analysis" and "Recommendations" respectively.

When writing your analysis, keep several factors in mind. First, your evaluations must be based solely upon your reported findings. No new supporting evidence can be introduced at this point.

Second, you do not always have the luxury of using deductive analysis. Sometimes you are forced to use inductive reasoning (see "Reason Rationally" on page 15). When you do induce, qualify your remarks with a phrase that alerts the readers to the fact that your conclusion is less than certain. ("Chances are . . .," or "It seems reasonable to conclude . . ." or "To the best of my knowledge . . ." are three illustrations.) When you can offer a more exact estimate ("There is a 90-percent likelihood . . ."), do so.

Third, if more supporting evidence is necessary to formulate a meaningful analysis, do not be too shy to confess "more research is necessary."

Fourth, be objective. Even the purest of thinkers have trouble overcoming their biases, expectations, and blind spots when evaluating evidence, so don't expect your quest for total objectivity to be child's play.

Your recommendations must be logically deduced or at least induced from your written analysis. When you suggest a course of action, be explicit. Specify who will do what to whom and when and where and why — and how. Should you give more than one recommendation, consider listing them chronologically or in order of their significance. Should you present alternative courses of action, frankly (or, if need be, subtly) indicate your favorite.

At times, the component that follows the "Body" of your report will not deal exclusively with conclusions or will not even present conclusions at all. In such cases, the heading "Conclusions" (or the co-headings "Analysis" and "Recommendations") would be a misnomer. One of the following headings would be more on target:

> "Summary of the Findings"
> "Summary of the Findings and Conclusions"
> "Summary and Conclusions"

"Summary of the Findings" is used when the report has no conclusions (as would be the case in a data-giving report) and the component following the "Body" is a more detailed digest of the findings than the one you offer in the "Introduction." This type of summary is appropriate for lengthy or involved data-giving reports. An alternative but less descriptive heading is "Summary."

"Summary of the Findings and Conclusions" is used when you digest the findings and conclusions discussed in the "Body." Again, an alternative but less descriptive heading is "Summary."

"Summary and Conclusions" is used when this component of your report comprises summarized material from the "Body" as well as conclusions that were not mentioned in the "Body."

WRITE THE APPENDIX

Among other possible titles for this part of your overall document are "Addendum" and "Supplementary Material." Use whatever title pleases you as long as it tells the readers what to expect.

Your appendix is a functional depository for information that would otherwise clutter the body of your document but which — nonetheless — is collateral evidence for your points and arguments. Typical nominees for the appendix are case histories, press clippings, reprints of pertinent articles, and lengthy statistical tables.

"Many are called but few are chosen" should be one of your mottos when determining what material should be incorporated in your appendix. If it is necessary to have a bulky appendix, package this support document in a binder or other suitable holder that is physically separate from your document proper. If your appendix is short, simply place it at the end of your document proper. At times, a pocket or envelope on the inside back cover of your document binder is the ideal receptacle (as might be the case for a series of small pamphlets or for appendix material that the readers will be consulting often as they read through your document).

Label your appendix and each of its subunits clearly. When you refer the reader to this material, use the exact title(s).

List the title of each subunit in your report's main contents or, if the subunits are many, in a special contents for the appendix. Situate the special contents immediately after the appendix's title page, and list only the term "Appendix" in the report's main contents.

WRITE THE BIBLIOGRAPHY

Your bibliography credits the published sources that you consulted while researching your report. Many formats exist. For an illustration of one of the most popular, see our own on page 225.

WRITE THE INDEX

An index gives your readers an alphabetical at-a-glance listing of names, places, and subjects mentioned or discussed in your report. It also specifies the pages where that material can be found. An index is usually necessary only for lengthy reports.

WRITE THE INFORMAL REPORT

The three basic informal reports are the:
Letter Report
Memo Report
Form Report
For a discussion on when to use these reports, see "Determine the Best Medium" on page 8.

WRITE THE LETTER REPORT

You will find a sample letter report on page 200.

Since a letter report is a letter, it should be typed on your letterhead and be dressed in all the customary garb of an everyday business letter: date line, inside address, salutation, body, complimentary closing, signature and your title (if it is not part of your letterhead). If they are needed, you can also add the attention line, subject line, initials of the dictator and typist, enclosure notation, and/or carbon-copy notation.

You are more likely to use headings in your letter reports than in your workaday letters (see "Write Effective Headings" on page 42). Headings are particularly beneficial when your letter report is lengthy and complex. Besides helping to break down your copy into easy-to-grasp units, headings can also make your letter more like a report.

While a formal report almost always has a cover letter to pave the way into the minds of the readers, a letter report never has one. In your letter report, therefore, you normally have to incorporate the "Here's the report" type of introduction and the "Thank you" and/or "If you need more information" type of closing that are illustrated in the first and last paragraphs in the "Sample Cover Letter" on page 22.

You are more likely to present your conclusions up front in a letter report than in a formal report. (See "Determine Which Goes First: The Evidence or Conclusions" on page 7). The best policy is: state your conclusions early in a letter report unless you have reason to do otherwise.

WRITE THE MEMO REPORT

See page 203 for a sample memo report.

The subject line has a gripping purpose: to describe to the reader as quickly as possible the gist of the report. Seldom should this line exceed ten words. If you can do it in even fewer words, all the better.

As with letter reports, most memo reports state the conclusions at or near the beginning of the document. Lengthy and complex memo reports can also profit from the use of headings. And memo reports usually should contain one or more of those features of a cover letter: "Here's the report" type of introduction, a thank you, and an offer to supply more information.

You do not necessarily have to sign a memo report. Doing so, however, gives your report a personal touch. Pen your signature or initials under the typed message. Or jot your initials immediately to the right of your typed name, which appears above the text.

WRITE THE FORM REPORT

A form report can vary in complexity from a single sheet of paper with a single question requiring a simple "yes" or "no" answer to a bureaucratic bundle of questions accompanied by capacious blank spaces for detailed commentary.

When designing the questions for a form report, state your requests for information in unequivocal terms. Accomplishing that objective is more easily said than done. You may know what you mean, but does the respondent in Oshkosh, Wisconsin? Take this example from a salesperson call report used by a major corporation:

> Where is the company
> located?_____
> _____
> _____

As simple as that question seems, it caused confusion. Some of the firm's new salespersons were unsure whether the question referred to the home or branch office of the company they visited. They were also uncertain as to whether they should list the entire address or merely the name of the city or town.

All doubt would have been eliminated if the person who composed the call report had viewed the question from the readers' vantage. He or she then might have asked the sales staff, "What is the full address of the company's home office?" A good idea is to test a form report for clarity on a representative sample before rolling it off the press.

Even if you can use the fear of being fired to force your respondents to complete the form report, limit your queries to only the most pertinent ones. The fewer questions they have to answer, the more conscientious their replies will be. Besides, filling out a form report takes time — company time.

If you receive a lot of routine reports and it is not practical to print a form report, consider writing a style sheet or manual to help insure that information in similar reports is uniformly presented. This style sheet would specify, for example, the type of data that should be collected and the format to use when submitting it.

WRITE THE TELEGRAM REPORT

A type of informal report that we have not yet discussed is the telegram (and its first cousins, the cable and mailgram) report. Because the cost of this type of medium varies according to the number of words used, most people expect and accept the absence of nonessential words such as "I," "the," and "please." This editorial license does not mean, however, that you can be excused for conveying hazy or nebulous thoughts. You must choose words and construct sentences that leave no doubt in your readers' minds. Precise nouns and verbs are crucial.

Word conservation also saves money when you send a telex report from one terminal to another, even though the charge is based on time rather than word count. Since the more words you use, the longer it will take to transmit your message, you may want to omit expendable words from a telex.

One tried and proven way to economize on words in a telegram or telex report is to establish with your readers prearranged codes for oft-said expressions. "Bid no more than . . ." could be condensed to "Bidmax. . . ."

WRITE SKILLFULLY

We present a number of gutsy writing hints in Parts Four and Five, "Common English Errors" and "Other Writing Guidelines," starting on pages 135 and 159 respectively.

DON'T BE AFRAID OF USING BOILERPLATE

Boilerplate is editorial material that you lift intact from one of your writings and insert into another of your writings. You employ this form of self-plagiarism to save time and the bother of having to express the same thoughts in different ways.

While the use of boilerplate is generally taboo when writing an article or book to be published, it often has a vital place in business writing. If, for instance, you are composing somewhat similar reports to be sent to twenty department heads within your company, you would be squandering company resources if you didn't borrow phraseology, sentences, and paragraphs from the first report you write and use them for the other reports. In short, customize when necessary and use pertinent boilerplate when it doesn't make a hoot of difference to your readers.

WRITE EFFECTIVE HEADINGS

Good headings are as important to your report as is good text. They help steer your readers through the report. They serve the same purpose as the overhead guides found in some office-building elevators, which tell passengers what they can expect to find on stepping out of the car. If a person is not interested, he or she need not waste time exploring a particular floor.

Your headings do more than guide. They make the report more inviting by breaking lengthy copy into bite-size pieces.

The text that follows a heading generally should be independent of the heading for its meaning. In other words, the text should be able to stand on its own two feet if the heading were eliminated.

Headings are classified by degree, a term that refers to their rank. There are headings of the first degree, second degree, third degree, and so on. Several heading systems exist that use this terminology.

For most business reports, the best heading system is the one that uses placement, capitalization, and underscoring to differentiate rankings. Unlike the classic and decimal heading (or outline) systems that we discuss later, it does not use letters or numbers for that purpose. When you use this system, you indicate a first-degree heading by centering it over the text and by typing it in solid capitals with no underscoring, as illustrated in the sample below. Specifications for second-, third- and fourth-degree headings are given with that sample.

FIRST-DEGREE HEADING

SECOND-DEGREE HEADING

       Locate a second-degree heading flush to the left margin and above the text. Type it in solid caps. It is usually underscored.

Third-Degree Heading

       Situate a third-degree heading as you would a second-degree heading, but type it in upper and lower cases. Always underscore it.

       Fourth-Degree Heading: Indent the fourth-degree heading and run it into the opening sentence of the text. Type it in upper and lower cases (or all lower case except the first letter of the first word). Follow it with a colon, dash, or period. Always underscore it.

When you use this heading system and you require only three degrees of headings, consider eliminating the third-degree heading style and substituting the style of the fourth-degree heading (as we do in this book). This modification is more appealing to the eye.

Yet another possibility is to eliminate the first-degree as well as third-degree headings, as we do in "Sample A: Formal Report" on page 189. Because the report has no chapters, we let the title page serve as the equivalent of a first-degree heading. In the text proper of the sample, we used only second- and fourth-degree headings.

The classic heading system — the one you probably were taught in school — is generally not used for business reports unless they are geared for the academic or scientific communities. The system is:

   I. First-Degree Heading
      A. Second-Degree Heading
      B. Second-Degree Heading
         1. Third-Degree Heading
         2. Third-Degree Heading
            a. Fourth-Degree Heading
            b. Fourth-Degree Heading
               (1) Fifth-Degree Heading
               (2) Fifth-Degree Heading
                  (a) Sixth-Degree Heading
                  (b) Sixth-Degree Heading
  II. First-Degree Heading

The decimal heading system, which is used even less frequently than the classic system in business reports, works like this:

1. First-Degree Heading
   1.1 Second-Degree Heading
   1.2 Second-Degree Heading
       1.21 Third-Degree Heading
       1.22 Third-Degree Heading
           1.221 Fourth-Degree Heading
           1.222 Fourth-Degree Heading
2. First-Degree Heading

Whatever heading system you use, remember that headings of the same degree should be consistent in terms of placement, capitalization, lettering, and numbering.

In addition, grammatical construction must be parallel for headings of the same degree. (In a full-length book, this rule applies only to headings within a given chapter. All chapter headings, however, must be consistent.) There are many ways in which a report writer can unthinkingly violate the rule for parallel construction. In the following illustration, notice how the first heading is a fragmentary and the second a complete sentence:

1. New Mining Equipment
2. The Mine Prospers

In our next illustration, the first heading is a command (imperative mood) and the second a declaration (indicative mood).

1. Assemble the Box
2. Filling the Box

Another example of non-parallel construction is the use of a question for one heading but not for another:

1. Which Is the Best Facility?
2. The Best Worker is Mrs. Polk

Report writers seem to be divided into two schools of thought when it comes to the issue of whether a heading should be highly descriptive and action-oriented. Writers for government agencies and conservative sectors of the business world generally prefer to use only a key word or phrase that identifies but does not describe the text.

1. Farm
   a. Labor
   b. Tractors
2. Dairy
   a. Cows
   b. Feed

In contrast, report writers in more progressive business fields usually opt for more evocative and action-oriented headings. Here's how they might recast the previous example:

1. Major Farm Trends
   a. Higher Labor Costs
   b. Larger, More Productive Tractors
2. Major Dairy Trends
   a. New Cow Breeds
   b. More Nutritious Feed

USE FOOTNOTES PROPERLY

Footnotes serve several purposes: to remove from your text ancillary material that may slow down your readers; to amplify a point; to refer readers to the original source of the information you present; to give editorial credit where credit is due — that is, when you have quoted or paraphrased someone or have borrowed someone else's unique thought or methodology. Excessive footnoting, however, can give your document a ponderous and pedantic character.

Some business reports list the footnotes at the end of the text proper. Although this method simplifies the typing chore for your secretary, we do not recommend it because it forces the reader to flip pages in order to look at a footnote entry. Footnotes are better placed at the bottom of their appropriate pages.

If you do not have a bibliography, you generally should give all the essentials for each citation, as we do in the sample footnote.[1] On the other hand, if you have a bibliography, you can abbreviate the footnote.[2]

When citing a source, you do not always have to use a footnote. If your citations are few, you may present them within your text. To illustrate:

> In the opinion of Dr. Markem ("Coal Forecasts," *Mining Industry Weekly*, May 8,

---

[1] *Future Chemistry* by Robyn Smith (Hudson Valley Press, New York, 1981), page 208.

[2] *Future Chemistry* by Robyn Smith, page 208.

1981, page 43), the economic outlook is excellent.

CREATE EFFECTIVE GRAPHIC AIDS

For a detailed discussion on preparing charts and other visual aids, see Part Three, "Graphic Aids," starting on page 99.

REDRAFT YOUR DOCUMENT

Virtually all of the world's great literary works, including those by Shakespeare and Goethe, were redrafted by their authors at least several times. If those word geniuses had to do it, so must lesser mortals.

Redrafting entails more than reorganizing the structure, adding missing vital details, increasing clarity, rectifying spelling and grammatical errors, and polishing the style. Redrafting also requires excising all extraneous data. It is not so much what the writer puts in as what he or she leaves out of the composition that distinguishes great reports from mediocre ones.

Deleting researched information that has already been scribed is one of the most trying tasks for a nonprofessional writer. There is, after all, a natural tendency not to want to kill one's brainchild. There is also a propensity among too many writers to be repetitious because they lack confidence in their ability to communicate an idea the first time around. They go around a concept as if they were in a revolving door.

Other reasons for not cropping words include these rationalizations that we have heard from otherwise skilled writers: "I have invested too much time in finding that piece of information not to use it." "The material will fatten my report and make it seem more impressive." "The extra bulk will disguise my lack of facts." "My readers expect a 100-page document." or "The extra pages will give my secretary something to do this afternoon."

Just as bad as glutting your document with words is going to the other extreme. If you over-edit, your writing style will smack of a telegram — cold and terse. There are times when some repetition is advisable, for instance, when you want to emphasize a key point. If the point is vital, you might want to adopt the time-honored orator's rule: First tell your audience what you're going to tell them, then tell them, and then tell them what you have just told them.

PROTECT THE CONFIDENTIALITY OF THE DOCUMENT

The readership of some reports must be restricted because, for instance, the documents contain trade secrets or marketing plans that shouldn't be read by your competition. To minimize the chance that someone within your company might inadvertently let such a report fall into the wrong hands, type or stamp wording along the lines of "Company confidential" or "Only for the eyes of . . ." above the title of the document.

Mark a document confidential only when absolutely necessary. Otherwise you'll lessen the clout of that word.

COPYRIGHT THE DOCUMENT IF NECESSARY

If there is reason to protect the editorial rights to your work, copyright it. The procedure is neither unduly difficult nor expensive.

First, before duplicating the document, you must place three essential items on the title page — or on a conspicuous place near the title page. These three necessary particulars are: the symbol © (or the word "copyright" or the abbreviation "copr."); the year the document was (or will be) first published or publicly released; the owner of the work. To illustrate: © 1981 by John Alexander.

In the meantime, if you do not already have one, request "The Application for Copyright Registration for a Nondramatic Literary Work" (Form TX) from the Register of Copyrights, Library of Congress, Washington, D.C. 20559. Return the completed form with a $10.00 check or money order and two copies of your published work (or one copy of your unpublished work). Within a few weeks the government-validated Form TX should be safely ensconced in your files.

Post-Writing Phase

Now that you have completed the final draft of your report, the time has come to type the document and get it into the hands of your readers.

Even if you have your secretary type the report (or a printer set it in type), there are certain basics you should know in order to supervise the task of giving the document an appealing appearance.

TYPE THE DOCUMENT

Neatness: Before readers actually study your document, they already will have formed an impression of it from its appearance. And that first impression can help determine how receptive they will be to what you have to say. A clean-looking document with an eye-appealing layout is inviting to read. Just as important, it conveys an air of professionalism and authority. Therefore, after investing time and energy to research and write your document, it does not make sense to allow anything to detract from its message. The paper, margins, indentations, spacings, page-numbering system — and typist — for your report should be selected with care.

Paper: A rag bond paper with at least a twenty-pound weight classification should be your choice because a heavy, quality paper tactually suggests that your report carries weight. It also better endures the handling that most reports suffer.

Margins: Wide margins attractively frame the text, thereby setting off your message. Ample white space also makes the document easier and more inviting to read. It follows that you should always leave plenty of room — at least one inch at the top and sides and one and one-half inches at the bottom of 8½ x 11-inch typing paper. (Single-spaced documents may need even wider margins in order that they not look cramped.) If your document will be bound, you must add about an extra three-quarters of an inch of space to the (left or top) margin where the binder will be.

Spacing: It is standard business practice to single-space letters and memos. This rule applies to reports (and proposals) in letter or memo form, as well as to cover letters for formal reports (and proposals). Formal reports should be double-spaced for ease of reading. Within a double-spaced document, however, quotations over three lines are single-spaced (and indented five spaces from the left and right margins). Contents, footnote, and bibliography entries that run two or more lines are single-spaced too.

Indentations: The main purpose of indentations is to help guide the readers by signaling the start of a new paragraph. If your document is double-spaced, your best bet is to use what is called the semi-block style. In this style, the first line in each paragraph is indented (usually five spaces) and paragraphs are separated from one another by four (or, less commonly, by three or two) lines. This combination leaves no doubt in the readers' minds about where paragraphs begin. If your document is single-spaced, you can use the semi-block (indent and skip two lines between paragraphs) or the block style.

In the block style, all lines begin directly at the left margin. Indenting is not considered necessary when the type is single-spaced because the eye can easily detect that paragraphs are separated by a double space. Indentations are used to distinguish fourth-degree headings (see page 43). In addition, quotes over three lines that appear in the text are usually indented five spaces from both the left and right margins.

Page Numbering: Documents of two or more pages should be numbered. Count every page in a letter or memo, but do not place a number on the first page. In a formal document, all pages except the cover, fly leaf (a blank sheet that is sometimes placed between the cover and title page), and title page are numbered. The title page should be counted as page one but not actually numbered. Use lower-case Roman numerals (i, ii, iii, iv, etc.) for the document's front matter and Arabic numerals (1, 2, 3, etc.) for the other pages. If your appendix is in a separate binding from the rest of the document, assign it its own Arabic numerals. Position numbers in the upper right-hand corner of each page if the document is to be bound or stapled on the left-hand side. Place them in the center bottom if the pages are to be bound or stapled at the top.

PROOF THE DOCUMENT

After the document is typed, the typist and you must painstakingly proof it and, if necessary, check it against the final draft. Because the typist and you are so familiar with the material at this point, there is a chance that you two will skip over a mistake or two. You may, therefore, want to have a third person peruse the pages for typos and grammatical errors. He or she should also be on the lookout for hazy thinking or lack of clarity, although at this stage there is little excuse for either. If it is your company's policy, be sure that all necessary internal approvals have been secured before releasing the document to an outside party.

DUPLICATE THE DOCUMENT

By now you should know exactly how many copies of the document you need. You obviously need one for each reader (unless you plan to circulate the document) and one or more for your own files. If there is only one primary reader, he or she should receive the original, which should be free of smudges, erasures, and other blemishes. If there is more than one reader, send the original to the person who is most important in terms of your document. When sending photocopies of a formal document to readers, you can personalize the parcel by sending each individual his or her own cover letter and by using an original title page, rather than a copy, for each report. If the report is not confidential and you have the permission of the person who assigned it, you may want to make extra copies to circulate around (or even beyond) your company. Some executives overlook the possibility that their documents can serve as enlightening in-house communications.

PACKAGE THE DOCUMENT

You don't have to be a marketing whiz to know the importance of packaging. If your formal document is lengthy or if you want to give it a more impressive air, bind it with a cover. After all, if the material is important enough to require a formal document, it should be significant enough to warrant a cover. When the document has a cover, it will also stay in better shape as it makes its rounds.

The title of your document must be visible on the front cover or on the spine. There is no problem if the cover is transparent and exposes the title page or if it has a window that reveals at least the title on the title page. However, if the front cover is opaque, you must affix or imprint the title on it or on the spine.

DELIVER THE DOCUMENT

You now have this perfect document in your hands. After all that work, you want to be certain that it ends up safely — and on time — in the hands of your readers.

If the readers are in your office or outside your organization but nearby, you may decide to show them how serious you believe your labor has been by delivering the document yourself. When this is impractical or unnecessary, you will have to relinquish your masterpiece to the care of your interoffice mail, a messenger service, or the U.S. Post Office. Before sending the document on its way, you or your secretary should double-check names and addresses to avoid having the document delayed or lost. Double-checking to see that all the proper contents are inside each envelope is a smart move too.

Whether you use a private service or the Post Office, protect your document with a strong, sturdy envelope. If you send your work through the U.S. Mail, be aware that certified mail with a request for a return receipt is as reliable for your purpose as is registered mail, but less expensive. Always try to mail your document early enough to meet the deadline in case the Post Office does not deliver it as quickly as it promises.

THINK OF FUTURE CONSEQUENCES

A poor report is a dormant volcano. It may not erupt right away, but when it does, some of the lava may flow in the direction of your desk.

Always put your best foot forward when you prepare a report because you never know who might eventually read your words. We know of a lamentable case where a naive junior executive gave his boss a report without stating the supporting evidence and reasoning for his unorthodox conclusions. He chose not to include those elements in his report because he had orally discussed them with the boss and was sure the boss remembered and went along with his arguments, which the boss did. Unfortunately, the boss decided to pass along the report to the president who, after reading the document, seriously questioned the analytical ability of the junior executive. The predicament could have been avoided with a brief summary of the evidence and reasoning or with a phrase such as "On the basis of the facts and logic we discussed in our meeting, I suggest that . . ."

Another lingering threat from the sleeping volcano is the possibility that a report can sit in someone else's files long after you have forgotten the existence of your written words. Recently we heard of a vice president whose hopes for promotion to the presidency of his firm were disrupted by his arch rival. The antagonist publicized some intemperate words from a seemingly inconsequential report that the vice president had penned early in his career. Once words are put down on paper and disseminated beyond your office door, it is nigh impossible to eradicate them.

Another place where a volcano can explode is in a court of law because business reports are increasingly being admitted as evidence in legal disputes. What you write today can influence a judge or jury tomorrow.

PART TWO

Proposal Writing

Introduction to Part Two

James T. Farrell, the author of the Studs Lonigan trilogy, lamented, writing is "one of the cruelest of professions." Certainly proposal writing is one of the cruelest of the writing disciplines because approximately ninety out of every one hundred proposals are rejected. Having your proposal snubbed is hard on the pocketbook — as well as on the ego — because the preparation of a proposal requires an investment in time. The answer to the problem of rejection obviously is not to stop writing proposals, but to increase the likelihood of their acceptance.

As with report writing, your undertaking will be more rewarding, as well as less costly and less toilsome, if you break it into three sequential phases. These phases — pre-writing, writing, and post-writing — are discussed separately in the following chapters.

Pre-writing Phase

A proposal is a sales instrument. Its unabashed mission is to induce (or, shall we say, seduce) the readers to follow a course of action favored by the writer. As successful salespersons know: you must do your homework before you pitch your prospect. Yet most proposal writers tend to become a little impatient, leaping into the writing phase before they take care of essential preliminaries. These include: knowing your reader; knowing your goals; assessing your chances; selecting the best medium, style, and length; drafting a tentative outline; developing a plan of action; doing the necessary research on the subject matter of your proposal.

KNOW YOUR READERS

Perhaps the most serious strategic blunder proposal writers commit is designing the proposal from the viewpoint of their own as opposed to the readers' needs. What those errant proposal scribes lack is reader orientation. After all, the proposal readers will not say "yes" simply because you are the greatest person or company in your field. What counts to the readers is how your proposal will benefit them — and how your proposal satisfies *their* rather than *your* priorities. In short, you must reverse roles. We cannot stress this precept enough.

By reversing roles, you are in a better position to identify the true needs of your readers — and until you have those needs in sharp focus, you won't be able to devise a meaningful solution to the readers' problems.

Pinpointing the needs is seldom a snap. Except in the instances of solicited proposals such as RFP's (Request for Proposal), the readers usually provide you with little more than a limited description of the problems they face. Sometimes you will receive a misleading statement, or perhaps none at all, because the readers of an unsolicited proposal often are oblivious to the existence or magnitude of their needs, or misconstrue their needs, or diagnose the symptoms and not the disease. (In those cases, your task is particularly difficult because you must not only discover the needs yourself, you must bring the readers around to accepting the validity of your revelation before you even attempt to offer your solution.)

In addition to getting a fix on the readers' needs, you must ascertain how much they already know — and how much more they need or want to know. Without these insights, you risk tempting fate by cranking into your proposal more or less data than is necessary.

It is valuable to know the degree of confidence the readers have in you. The more of an unknown or questionable quantity you are to them, the more you need to substantiate your case. In contrast, if your reputation with the readers is stellar, a glut of documentation may cause them to call to mind Hamlet's declaration, "The lady doth protest too much, methinks."

Most proposal recipients have two faces — the public and the private one. A major feature of the private face is personal ambition. "Self-interest speaks all sorts of tongues and plays all sorts of roles" is as true in today's business realm as it was when the cynical duke François de La Rochefoucauld penned it in the seventeenth century. How much of a role will job security, for example, play in the readers' final decision? What about career or power aspirations? Intra-office rivalry? In the real corporate world, all these and other forms of self-interest help mold the ultimate "yes" or "no" decision.

Determine if there is anyone within or in contact with the readers' organization who may try to scuttle your proposal ship. If so, this early intelligence gives you the awareness and time that will be needed if you are to disarm any potential adversary. Defuse bombs before they explode.

Your search for possible enemies can also reveal potential advocates, individuals within the readers' organization who can put in a good word on behalf of your proposal. Once again, through early identification, you gain time to develop the goodwill and cooperation as well as the support of people who hold sway over the outcome of your proposal.

KNOW YOUR GOAL

Being cognizant of what the readers need is essential but insufficient. You must also have a lucid perception of what you want to accomplish. Without that goal awareness, your attempt to develop a match-up between what the readers want done and what you want to do will be a hit-or-miss affair.

A precise goal definition has other advantages. If you do not have a clear picture of what you want to do, how will the proposal readers grasp your intent and, therefore, how will they be able to judge wisely whether your propositions will solve their specific needs? Just as critical, a nebulously stated goal creates doubt in the readers' minds about your level of professionalism.

You derive yet another benefit from a precisely stated goal. Only with one can you intelligently draft the basic elements of your proposal, such as methods and budget, because if those components are to be sound, they must be logical outgrowths of your objective.

A trenchant goal helps to safeguard your future in more than one way. First, it lets you see if the proposition compromises your long-term goals. Second, a well-defined goal greatly increases the likelihood that you and the readers will be following the same set of ground rules, and therefore decreases the chances of a misunderstanding once the proposal is accepted. Your clarity also gives the readers less opportunity to change — for sake of expediency — their interpretation of the ground rules as time progresses.

If a goal is well defined, the writer should be able to express it in a sentence or, at most, in a short paragraph or two. If the writer cannot, we dare say that his or her conception of what he or she wants to accomplish is still fuzzy.

Condensing your goal description into a few words requires more than an inspired sweep of the pen. During World War II, Winston Churchill was asked by a club if he could give an hour's talk on how England hoped to defeat Hitler. When the cigar-chomping Prime Minister politely told the group leader that he had to decline because he did not have the time to write the speech, she inquired whether he could deliver a half-hour oration. Churchill promptly demurred, "But a thirty-minute address on that topic would take twice as long to prepare as one of sixty minutes."

Should you have a hard time verbalizing your goal, scratch it out on a blank piece of paper, even if your incipient ideas are muddled. It is easier to polish thoughts once they have been recorded on paper. Moreover, you can circulate that inscribed goal for possible constructive criticisms from your colleagues, who probably are not as close to the proposal as you are and who therefore may be able to give you valuable perspective.

ASSESS YOUR CHANCES OF SUCCESS

Oscar Wilde defined horse sense as the prudence that keeps horses from betting on people. Horse sense is also the wisdom of not wasting time and money researching, writing, and submitting a proposal when the track odds do not justify the bet. In those circumstances, the proposal writer's limited stakes (who has an unlimited bank roll?) would be better wagered in greener pastures.

To minimize the possibility of backing the wrong horse, make a hard-nosed analysis of the chances of your proposal being accepted. This can be done, of course, only after you have zeroed in on the readers' needs and on your own goal.

The greater your unique selling proposition, the better your chances. Unique selling proposition (USP), simply defined, is those aspects of your products or services that are better than the competition's. Singling out your USP is not as easy as it may seem because it is often hard to make an objective survey of your own position within a field of rivals. For the needed perspective, ask a cross section of informed people outside your organization for their candid views of your relative strengths and weaknesses in your professional sphere.

You must also ask yourself questions such as "Does my competition have an inside track because of special conditions that have nothing to do with merit?" "Do my readers share my appraisal of my reputation and capability?"

Then compare your new assessment of your gamble with the expected returns. All this should be done before you plunk down your money and certainly before the starter's buzzer mechanism opens the starting gate, allowing your filly to race unrestrained towards the finish line.

SELECT THE BEST MEDIUM, STYLE, AND LENGTH

The factors that you should consider when choosing the medium, style, and length for your proposal are practically the same ones you must take into account when writing a report. Rather than repeat the information, we refer you to the following sections in Part One:

Determine the Best Medium (page 8)
Determine the Most Appropriate Style (page 9)
Determine the Ideal Length (page 11)

DRAFT A TENTATIVE OUTLINE OF THE PROPOSAL

If your analysis indicates that the potential reward will justify the cost of preparing the proposal, you are ready to draft a tentative outline of that proposal. (You'll find format suggestions in the next chapter, "Writing Phase.") At this juncture, the selection and logical arrangement of the components of the outline are infinitely more important than the words you choose to express your ideas. Your immediate objective is to build a trial superstructure for your inchoate proposal so that you can test the soundness of its framework and, if necessary, make suitable modifications. Your outline also serves two other purposes: it enables you to design a practical plan of action and it gives you organized pigeonholes for data that you research.

DEVELOP A PLAN OF ACTION

Before starting the actual research, devise your plan of action. It should specify who will do what to whom — and when, where, and why — during the period when the proposal will be researched, written, and submitted. Anticipated or feared setbacks and bottlenecks as well as costs should be set forth.

A plan of action must be consistent with what your organization realistically can and cannot do. We've seen hundreds of plans of action that have falsely assumed, for instance, that a particular person within the writer's organization would be willing or able to contribute his or her time or that the designated person had the needed knowhow.

You need not prepare an intricate plan of action if the proposal's subject matter is relatively uncomplicated, especially if you are the sole orchestrator. A more involved proposal and/or one that requires the interaction of a number of people, on the other hand, calls for a sophisticated game plan complete with a timetable if efficiency is to be attained and potential personnel conflicts within an organization are to be minimized. As any leprechaun will tell you, another variable that influences the elaborateness of your plan of action is the size of the pot of gold at the end of the rainbow.

DO THE NECESSARY RESEARCH ON THE SUBJECT MATTER OF YOUR PROPOSAL

The business firmament is studded with dim stars, those proposal writers who try to explain to others what they do not understand themselves. Because their research is insufficient, they write around the subject, seldom penetrating its core. The resulting proposals are confusing and tedious, suffering from a flood of words and a trickle of substance.

Proposals are also frequently marred by slipshod research, the result of poor methodology, slapdash note-taking and record keeping, or faulty reasoning. Readers detect those defects more often than many scribes suspect.

In terms of cost-effectiveness, if a proposal is worth writing, it is generally worth researching well. The extra time and money you spend to do a diligent as opposed to a so-so research job is usually more than compensated for by the increased chances of your proposal being accepted. Good research is a good investment.

You should consider the paralyzing long-term effects on your good name should the readers find the quality or quantity of your research wanting. Because your document becomes a conspicuous record, your neck is on the corporate chopping block. Better to use your head than lose it.

Take the time to set up a workable system for collecting and storing the data you will research. If well-conceived and -executed, the process makes your proposal-preparation task quicker, easier, and less irksome. It also helps assure you a higher quality proposal because you will have at your disposal a greater arsenal of potent facts for supporting your premises and drawing your conclusions. Oh, how often has a proposal writer researched a convincing fact that could not be found or called to mind when it was needed!

If a number of people will be contributing to or using the information system, then the responsibility and authority for maintaining it, as well as for providing direction for the overall proposal-writing effort, usually should be placed in the hands of one individual. Committees formed for these purposes tend to keep minutes and waste hours.

Not all the data you gather during your research is necessarily factual. More than likely some of your accumulated information is based partially or totally on assumption. Perhaps your research effort is hampered by time or budgetary limitations — or maybe it is hobbled by the unavailability of facts that you need. In those cases, at least make an attempt to test your assumptions with the intended readers of your proposal before you irretrievably submit the document.

Communication with the readers before you write the final draft of your proposal can furnish you with feedback that will allow you to make necessary adjustments in the structure or approach of your proposal. That feedback may even show you that the idea of preparing a proposal is folly because the people you are courting would not accept your proposal — or, if they did, they would do so only in a way that would be unprofitable for you or would force you to compromise your long-term goals. This form of negative feedback is actually beneficial because it can stop you from investing more time and money pursuing a quarry that you shouldn't be stalking in the first place.

Writing Phase

Pity the many hapless souls whose splendid ideas are rejected because they do not know how to translate their concepts into persuasive written proposals. We use the word "pity" because the skill of writing proposals can be learned.

A well-written proposal is indispensable because, when the decision-making readers sit down to review the merits of your proposition, that document will likely be your only representative in attendance. You will not be able to respond in person to the questions of the moment. Nor will you be able to counter objections as they are raised. Should your proposal mold the wrong impression or be equivocal or fact-starved, your prospects will be severely dampened.

A proposal, if it is to be a good one, will take time to write. Granted, there are individuals who brag about their lightning-fast ability to crank out proposals to clients by cutting and pasting together previous proposals, linking the parts with rhetoric. When their proposals win, the victory nearly always rightfully belongs to the excellence of their organization and the idea and not, as those wordsmiths are wont to vaunt, to their writing genius. The issue here is whether their success rate could be raised even higher if their documents were more deliberately prepared.

Proposal writing, however, need not be inordinately time-consuming. Neither does it have to be mentally anguishing. Your writing chore is always quicker and easier when you break it down into manageable pieces.

SELECT THE BEST FORMAT

Once you have mastered the format for a formal proposal, you will be able to design the perfect format for practically any type of proposal. After all, letter and memo proposals are abridged formal proposals. We therefore devote the next twelve sections to the formal-proposal format.

PICTURE THE FORMAL PROPOSAL IN PERSPECTIVE

A proposal has four fundamental parts:
> Cover letter
> Title page
> Text proper
> Addendum

As you can see when comparing this list to the list for reports on pages 19-20, the names for two of the parts are different. The phrase "title page" is more appropriate than "front matter" for proposals because they seldom contain more than a title page as front matter. The term "addendum" is more appropriate than "back matter" because proposals rarely have more than addendum material as back matter.

The text proper of a classic formal proposal has eight components:

> I.   Introduction and Summary
> II. The Need
> III. The Objective
> IV. The Methods
> V.   The Proposer's Qualifications

VI. The Evaluation
VII. The Budget
VIII. The Program's Future

Naturally, some formal proposals do not need all eight components. For instance, a proposal to switch the company's observance of the Columbus Day holiday from Thursday to Friday would not require a budget. Neither would it need "The Proposer's Qualifications," "The Evaluation," or "The Program's Future."

All proposals — be they formal, letter, or memo — must contain these three components: "the need," "the objective," and "the methods." This rule is true whether or not the writer uses the labels "need," "objective," and "methods."

These three components must flow, without exception, in this logical sequence:

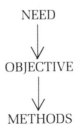

NEED

OBJECTIVE

METHODS

The first component, "the need," determines "the objective," which in turn determines "the methods." In other words, the methods must be predicated on the objective, which in turn, must be based on the need. To fashion the objective before pinpointing the need would be putting the cart before the horse. The same is true for designing your methods before you have your objective clearly in mind.

The cover letter, title page, eight components of the text proper, and the addendum are discussed in the sections that follow.

WRITE THE COVER LETTER

Even though this letter is the first part of your proposal, you should write it after you have drafted your text proper and addendum. (However, if your proposal is in a letter or memo format, there is no need to write it at all.)

While the proper length for your cover letter is only a page or less, you should invest ample time in drafting it because the evaluators will probably read it before any other part of your proposal. Not only do first impressions help influence how much interest and time the evaluators will want to devote to the study of your total proposal, first impressions also can sway the readers' final judgment. A well-designed cover letter also helps orient the readers and thus reduces the risk of their misunderstanding the thrust of your proposition.

The nucleus of your cover letter is a condensation of the "Introduction and Summary" component of your proposal — and if you have soundly developed that component, the words for your cover letter should flow off your pen. Your cover letter should succinctly and objectively state your proposition and the reason(s) your readers will benefit if they accept it. You must also summarize your credentials, convey genuine enthusiasm, and offer to supply any further information that the readers may desire.

Try to make sure that your opening paragraph contains wording that is obviously customized (such as a reference to

SAMPLE COVER LETTER

Dear Mrs. Woodling:

  I am pleased to submit to your firm, Cargo-Air, our proposal for reducing your in-transit theft losses. As we discussed over lunch, you can reduce your firm's pilferage cost by $73,000 a year by leasing 125 of our Firmseal aluminum containers at a total cost of $51,250 per year. This savings represents a $21,750 increase in your annual profits.

  Our Firmseal containers have been successfully field-tested by other air carriers, including Air Freight America. I am very confident that you, too, will become a very satisfied customer.

  We can deliver the containers to you by December 31 if you place your order by September 30. Please let me know if you need any additional information.

  I look forward to your order.

         Sincerely,

---

a previous dialogue you had with the readers). This tactic illustrates to the readers that you have taken the time to learn something about them and/or their needs. You might also want to include in the letter a thank you or two for their assistance, but forgo the style epitomized by the acceptance speeches of Academy Award winners.

If your proposal has a "kicker" (an enticement that will encourage the readers to take prompt action), it does no harm to incorporate it in your cover letter. In our sample cover letter on page 75, the kicker is "We can deliver . . . by December 31 . . . if you . . . order by September 30."

Keep your cover letter brief. If the reader of your proposal is your immediate supervisor and he or she is already aware of the nature of your proposal, you sometimes need do no more than scribe on a small memo sheet a phrase such as "Here is my proposal for reorganizing the department." When the proposal is directed outside your organization, use your company's letterhead.

With few exceptions, the cover letter and proposal should have identical dates. In addition, the signatory of the cover letter and proposal should be one and the same person.

WRITE THE TITLE PAGE

Most of the tips and insights that we give on writing a title page for reports are also valid for proposals. Therefore review that topic starting on page 23. Also glance at the layout for a title page in "Sample D: Formal Proposal" on page 205. In addition, study the following two guidelines that specifically apply to proposals.

Your title should describe the crux of your overture from the readers' point of view. This principle is illustrated by comparing this title:

a proposal
TO LEASE
THE BJ-1000 COMPUTER
TO MID-AMERICA FOUNDRY INC.
AT $50,000 PER YEAR

With this title:

a proposal
TO REDUCE
BY $10,000 A YEAR
THE DATA-PROCESSING COST
OF MID-AMERICA FOUNDRY INC.

While BJ Computer's aim is to lease a computer to the foundry, the underlying need of the foundry is not to lease a computer but rather to reduce data-processing costs. Therefore the second title is more effective.

When money is involved, one of the first questions an executive asks is, "How much is it going to save or cost me?" Do not be uneasy about conspicuously displaying the dollar figure on the title page (as well as in the opening paragraph of your introduction and summary). By burying the amount in your document, you may lead your readers to the conclusion that you think the saving inconsequential or the expense exorbitant.

WRITE THE "INTRODUCTION AND SUMMARY" COMPONENT

Even though your "Introduction and Summary" component is the first of the eight components of your proposal proper, do not write it until after you have drafted your way through the remaining seven components, from "The Need" to "The Program's Future."

The ultimate purpose of your "Introduction and Summary" component is to allow the readers to determine instantly whether your proposition will solve their needs. If their conclusion is "no," they don't have to waste further time poring through your document. If their judgment is "yes," they will review the individual facets of your proposal with greater perspective and heightened interest, two qualities that will increase the chances that your proposal will be given a fair shake.

Your "Introduction and Summary" component should spotlight the key points you make in the other components. Boldly lead off with your proposition. It does not have to be more than a slightly expanded adaptation of your proposal's title. Then quickly explain to your readers why they need what you are offering. When describing this need, be sure you stress its significance and urgency. Tell your readers how you plan to satisfy their needs and why you are uniquely qualified to do so.

Your choice of words, tone, and facts will do much to build or destroy a reader's confidence in you. Because this component is the gateway to your proposal, establishing credibility at this juncture is especially important.

Keep the "Introduction and Summary" component short, as its title implies. One rule of thumb is not more than five hundred words or 10 percent of the length of the narrative, whichever is less. (Of course, if your entire proposal is only several hundred words long, you can omit this component.)

Saying what you want to say about your proposal in the short confines of your "Introduction and Summary" component is not the easiest of tasks. In order to make sure that you *do* keep it within bounds, you must mercilessly conserve words. Relegate everything but the brightest highlights to later components where they belong. If you have a "maintenance-free gizmo," say no more at this point but detail what you mean by "maintenance-free" in the appropriate component.

Should you still have difficulty paring your "Introduction and Summary" component to its proper size, call to mind what the renowned Broadway producer David Belasco said, "If you can't write your idea on the back of my calling card, you don't have a clear idea."

WRITE "THE NEED" COMPONENT

The primary purpose of "The Need" component is to make certain the readers recognize the need that you propose to satisfy. Unless you convince them of the magnitude, relevancy, and urgency of their need, the rest of your proposal will be immaterial to them.

If you did your research in the pre-writing phase, you should have a fairly good idea of how clearly your readers perceive their need. Consequently, there should be little reason for falling into the trap of assuming that they fully appreciate the significance of the need when they do not. Neither should there be any excuse for you to ramble on and on, telling the readers what they already know. If your proposal is of the solicited variety, you need do no more than briefly state the need — that is, unless you have uncovered crucial ramifications that you believe to be unknown to your readers. In that case, because you have unearthed pieces of the problem that they may have overlooked, you must broach your revelations diplomatically to avoid embarrassing your readers. Tread lightly on this perilous ground.

Define the parameters of the need. Sometimes you may choose to concentrate on a particular need of the readers that is actually part of their greater problem. Your rationale for this decision may be that there is a limit to how much of the overall need your organization can meet in terms of time and resources. Just remember to communicate to the readers that you are aware of how your piece fits into the mosaic, lest they think you do not see the realistic priority of your proposal in relation to their big picture.

Except in the case of a solicited proposal, you will probably have to do more than articulate the need. Likely, you also will have to document your claims with facts and informed opinions. You could, for example, give the names of authorities who can substantiate the validity of your data and analysis. (Of course, you should first secure permission from those experts.) Another procedure is to slip into your addendum verification letters from those individuals. You could also refer the readers to collaborating data that is available elsewhere. You have many options.

WRITE "THE OBJECTIVE" COMPONENT

"Objective" and "Methods" are different components. Yet most proposal writers unknowingly confuse them. The distinction between the two terms can be made clear with this definition: your "Objective" is what you want to accomplish, while your "Methods" are the steps you will take to achieve that objective. Stated another way: your "Methods" will be your means to the end, while your "Objective" is that end itself.

A proposal writer, therefore, would be in error if he or she said, "Our objective is to redesign the hydroelectric system of Rock Creek Dam." That statement deals with methods. The proposal writer should have penned, "Our objective is to increase the power output of Rock Creek Dam."

There is an important advantage to making sure you are telling the readers the objective rather than the methods at this stage of your proposal. An objective better arouses the interest of the readers because it divulges how they will benefit. As seasoned sales executives have long taught their trainees, it is usually more effective "to sell the sizzle than the steak." This advice means to emphasize the expected benefits rather than items such as equipment or abstract thoughts such as processes.

If a proposition is worth its salt, then its objective — with rare exception — should meet five criteria. First, it must be a natural outgrowth of the needs. Second, it should benefit both the proposer and the proposee. Third, it should be attainable (Do you, for instance, have the needed horses in terms of time and resources?).

Fourth, it should be practical. Decreasing plant theft by hiring a small army of armed guards is certainly attainable, but could the necessary funds for the project be put to better use elsewhere?

Finally, the objective should be measurable. In the case of the armed guards, could the difference between the cost of the program and the reduction in losses due to theft be estimated? Naturally, some objectives are easier to quantify than others. For instance, it is much easier to measure with precision an increase in profits than it would be to determine an increase in employee goodwill.

At times you may have more than one objective. Generally you should state them in order of their importance to the readers because your choice of sequence tells them something of your sense of priority. There are certain situations, however, that call for a chronological progression.

WRITE "THE METHODS" COMPONENT

In the previous component you told your readers the objective. Now you must detail how you plan to achieve that objective — and why your chosen set of methods is preferable to many other alternatives. If the selected methods are less than excellent, then even the glibbest of proposal writers would find it nigh impossible to camouflage the deficiency.

Even if you have superior methods, you must prove your case. You may, for example, assure the reader that you are aware of all the serious options and that you understand the strengths and weaknesses of each. You may also show that you recognize the potential stumbling blocks and know how to circumvent or overcome them. In our illustration of the hydroelectric generator for the dam (page 81), the proposal writer may have to address the looming problem of possible labor disputes resulting from layoffs due to the increased efficiency of the redesigned generator.

One of many possible ways to present your supporting evidence is to cite authorities. Or, you could note how you or someone else has successfully used the types of methods that you are proposing.

Your "Methods" component should spell out factors such as who will do what — and where, how, and to whom. For instance, name the individuals (or titles of these individuals) who will be delegated the responsibility and authority for each critical activity. Enumerate and describe the major pieces of equipment that will be employed. Specify time periods. State deadlines.

When setting deadlines, be realistic. Since time immemorial people have tended to underestimate how long it will take to get a job done. We see no reason why this trait won't continue to be a bane of most of the proposals that will be written in the coming years.

The more professionally you present your methods, the more competent you will seem and the more confidence the readers will have in you. One way to accomplish this goal is to present your methods in a verbal or graphic step-by-step timetable format. Most readers relish this approach because it allows them to perceive swiftly the chronological sequence of your methods. A timetable also makes your priorities more evident.

With the possible exception of "The Budget" component, this component will be the longest one in your proposal. The exact length will be a function of several factors, including the readers' desires and your proposition's degree of technical complexity. As always, when in doubt, favor brevity.

WRITE "THE PROPOSER'S QUALIFICATIONS" COMPONENT

Don't hide your light under a bushel. It doesn't make any difference how bright your qualifications are if your readers don't see the light. All too many proposal writers play down their qualifications either out of false modesty or because they mistakenly believe that the readers are aware of these merits. We do not mean to suggest, however, that you use too big a lantern as that tactic could cause your bushel to catch fire and go up in smoke. You must strike a proper balance between keeping your readers in the dark and blinding them with your sheer brilliance.

Your goal in this component is to forge confidence and credibility. You want to assure the readers that you have the skills and wherewithal to satisfy their needs — and that you are the most capable of the individuals or organizations with whom you may be in competition.

Recount your strengths, not your rivals' weaknesses. Highlight your track record. If your organization is new, accent what the key staff members accomplished before they joined your team. When describing the personnel, give only biographical sketches and present only those details that have a direct bearing on the project. General background items, such as those that fatten a résumé or vita, belong — if anywhere — in your addendum.

Specify relevant equipment, facilities, information sources, and contacts. Consider giving the names, addresses, and telephone numbers of third-party individuals who have agreed to verify your claims. Or place testimonial letters in your addendum.

Select for this component a title that suits your particular purposes. "Our Qualifications" and "Qualifications of (your organization's name)" are two of a wide variety of choices.

WRITE "THE EVALUATION" COMPONENT

Only special types of formal proposals require "The Evaluation" component. Those proposals are usually for research or public-service projects where the funder wants meaningful criteria by which to measure how well the project accomplished its objective.

An evaluation program does more than give standards by which to assess the degree of success of your project when it is completed. It tests whether your objective is measurable (see "Write 'The Objective' Component" on page 80). An evaluation program also provides a tool that enables you to judge your proposal in midcourse, thereby allowing you to ascertain whether practicality dictates that you modify your objective and methods before you finish your project.

Your chosen criteria for measuring success should be as objective as possible. Assume that your objective is to increase the use of the employee cafeteria (by redecorating the dining room, your method). If you plan to measure employee satisfaction with the cafeteria before and after the proposed undertaking, then you are using a subjective criterion. If you plan to compare attendance or sales figures before and after the proposed undertaking, then you are using an objective criterion. To add even greater objectivity to your evaluation program, consider asking an impartial person to administer your evaluation system.

WRITE "THE BUDGET" COMPONENT

A budget is your methods stated in dollars and cents. It's as simple as that.

Naturally, not all proposal budgets need to be as detailed or methodically presented as the one we discuss below. If you are charging your client a fixed fee, perhaps all you will have to say is "My total fee is $100,000." If you are going to bill your client on a "fixed fee plus" basis, then you might write, "My fee is $75,000 plus the cost of out-of-town travel." (Of course, in the latter case, you probably wouldn't be able to get away with just saying, "out-of-town travel." Your client would most likely want to know what you mean by "out-of-town travel" and what you think the costs will be.)

Even if your budget is stated as briefly as "My fee is $100,000," you have to know how to construct a budget in order to minimize the risk of underestimating or overestimating costs. The first error can cost you profits while the second mistake can cost you the prize. Either miscalculation can damage your professional reputation.

Some proposal writers automatically pad their budgets in the belief that the evaluators will automatically trim whatever figures are presented to them. Unless you are certain that the readers habitually use their pruning shears, keep your figures realistic because the majority of proposal evaluators can detect embellished estimates.

The length of a budget component for most formal proposals is roughly one or two single-spaced typewritten pages. The exact length should be determined mainly by the nature and complexity of your proposition and the desires of your readers. If, for instance, your proposal is for a standardized project or is directed at readers who are very knowledgeable about the methods you have chosen, you probably need not present more than budgetary highlights. Travel expenditures, salaries, consulting fees, and other costs that tend to raise the skeptical eyebrows of readers usually demand more details and rationalization than do expenses such as rent.

When your budget spans beyond a year's duration, you normally give more detail to the first year than you do to the ensuing years. Your calculations for future expenditures should be adjusted according to the forecasted rate of inflation. Also take into consideration anticipated merit raises.

Whether you are preparing a single- or multi-year budget, if it unavoidably becomes long and cumbersome, move some of the less vital details into your addendum.

An expensive mistake is underestimating the time necessary for an employee to finish a job. If your estimate is too conservative and your budget is unchangeable, you may have to pay for wage and salary cost overruns out of your general budget.

The possible variations in budget formats are legion. Unless you or your readers have a preference for a particular format, use our ten-category outline as a model:

PERSONNEL
OUTSIDE SERVICES
RENT
UTILITIES
EQUIPMENT
SUPPLIES
TRAVEL AND MEETINGS
MISCELLANEOUS EXPENSES
GENERAL RESERVE
INDIRECT COSTS

Modify the categories to fit the unique nature of your proposition. If your subcategory for the purchase of hydro-electric generators is fairly large, consider giving it its own category rather than burying the expense with other expenses in the "Equipment" category. By the same token, if the budget for your "Outside Services" category is scant, you should probably eliminate that category and list the expense in either the "Personnel" or "Miscellaneous Expenses" category.

In our sample formal proposal, the budget component beginning on page 213 illustrates how the ten categories are presented on paper. Refer to that sample as you read the following subsection which gives specific tips and insights on the ten budget categories.

Personnel — Chances are that more of your budget dollars will settle into this category than into any other. If your project is one that performs a service, it is possible that your personnel category will comprise nearly all of your budget. The personnel category is often subdivided into two parts: "salary and wages" and "fringe benefits." The latter component includes expenditures such as social security, unemployment insurance, health insurance, and private retirement insurance. Those benefits can be itemized, or if it is acceptable to your readers, can be figured as a percentage (usually 10 to 20 percent) of salary and wages.

Outside Services — Accounting, legal, and public-relations consulting fees, as well as expenses for the services of a free-lance photographer, are illustrations of the type of cost recorded in this category.

Rent — You will not have to include a rent category if rental expense will be calculated as part of your indirect costs category.

Utilities — Place into this category expenses such as telephone calls and telexes. Also include water, gas, and electricity if they are not buried within the rent or indirect-cost category.

Equipment — The dividing line between "Equipment" and "Supplies" is often arbitrarily drawn. The majority of proposal writers prefer to list a physical object within the "Equipment" category if it has a life-span of at least one year and/or has a value of at least $100 or $200. If a piece of equipment has a useful life beyond the proposed project, you would normally assign a fair and reasonable portion of its overall cost to your proposal budget. For instance, if a new $25,000 photocopier has a five-year life-span, you would probably assign up to half of that figure to a one-year proposal budget because of the depreciation factor. When your proposal is directed at an outside organization, you can sidestep a potential dispute by making sure that, if applicable, you clearly state that you will be the owner of the equipment at the project's completion.

Supplies — Itemize supplies such as postage stamps and stationery if the cost is relatively significant. Lump together less expensive items such as paper clips, pencils, rubber bands, and the like.

Travel and Meetings — To nip in the bud any reader's suspicion that you are going off on an extravagant pleasure trip, it is usually necessary to present a little extra detail in this category. The expense for an extended trip to a faraway city, for example, should be itemized into subcategories such as "airfare" and "seminar fee." Check with the evaluators to see if you can list hotel, food, and/or local transportation expenses on a per diem basis.

Miscellaneous — This catchall category is ideal for those budgetary items that do not logically fall into another category and that have a dollar value too insignificant to justify creating a new category.

General Reserve — It is the way of the world that no matter how carefully you plan your budget, unexpected expenses usually rear their ugly heads when and where you least expect them. Some evaluators allow the proposal writer to indicate a "General Reserve" category to cover contingency expenses, usually figured as a percentage of the overall budget. You can usually use a rate as high as 5 percent. (A higher percentage rightfully suggests that the proposal writer did not devote enough time and thought to estimating the various individual items in the budget.)

Indirect Costs — At times, your readers or the nature of your project will demand that you divide the costs in your budget into two categories: direct and indirect. Direct costs are those that are incurred as a direct result of your project. Indirect costs are those that will occur whether or not your project is undertaken. The rent for the space your department occupies at corporate headquarters is a likely example of indirect costs. Another illustration is the portion of your corporate officers' salaries that can be allocated to your department.

Normally you state your indirect cost rate as a percentage of the overall direct costs (or, sometimes, of the total salaries). If you and your intended proposal recipients agree that the appropriate percentage figure is 25 percent, and your direct costs are $300,000, then you would include in your budget $75,000 for indirect costs. Determining some indirect costs as a percentage of direct costs is practical because it would be ludicrous, for instance, to estimate and state that your corporate finance officer's secretary will devote $76.43 worth of time to your project.

Certain costs fall unequivocably into either the direct or indirect category. The salary of the assistant project director is an example of the first and that of the company's janitorial staff illustrates the second type. Some expenses such as fringe benefits are less easy to categorize as one or the other. Flip a coin if you must, but once you take a position be consistent.

WRITE "THE PROGRAM'S FUTURE" COMPONENT

If, for any number of reasons, your project will extend beyond the period budgeted in your proposal, consider including "The Program's Future" component. This situation might occur, for instance, if you are seeking funding to research and develop a new commercial soap product. You might explain to the readers how the intelligence that you will gather during the project at hand will enable you to develop other solvents in the future.

WRITE THE APPENDIX

The guidelines given in the "Write the Appendix" section for reports also apply to proposals. See page 35.

WRITE THE LETTER AND MEMO PROPOSALS

For a sample letter proposal and a sample memo proposal, see pages 216 and 218 respectively. Also see the relevant information in "Write the Letter Report" on page 37 and "Write the Memo Report" on page 38.

CONSULT OTHER PARTS OF THIS BOOK

Elsewhere in this volume you will find other valuable tips and insights that will help you write better proposals.

For instance, some of the pointers that we give for reports are equally valid for proposals. Rather than repeat ourselves, we refer you to the following sections in the "Writing Phase" for reports in Part One starting on page 41:

Don't Be Afraid of Using Boilerplate
Write Effective Headings
Use Footnotes Properly
Redraft Your Document
Protect the Confidentiality of Your Document

Also study these parts of our book:

Part Three — Graphic Aids
Part Four — Common English Errors
Part Five — Other Writing Guidelines

Post-Writing Phase

You have a sense of satisfaction — not to mention relief — as you put the pencil down after finishing the final draft of your proposal. Don't feel too content just yet. There's still plenty of work to be done.

TYPE, PROOF, DUPLICATE, PACKAGE, AND DELIVER THE PROPOSAL

The lion's share of guidelines we give for typing, proofing, duplicating, packaging, and delivering reports are valid for proposals too. We refer you to the following sections in the "Post-Writing Phase" of reports, starting on page 51:

> Type the Document
> Proof the Document
> Duplicate the Document
> Package the Document
> Deliver the Document

CONSIDER THE LEGAL IMPLICATIONS

Many proposal writers forget that a proposal to an outside firm becomes legally binding once it is accepted. Before you release the proposal, be absolutely certain that you can fulfill all the promises it makes. Also examine the document for loopholes that may allow the acceptor to alter the original intent of the deal or to squirm out of it altogether.

INQUIRE IF YOU DO NOT RECEIVE WORD

Sometimes you submit a proposal and do not receive an acknowledgment that it reached the proper hands. If this is the case, you should probably make an inquiring phone call (or send a letter) just to make sure the document arrived.

If the readers are unreasonably slow in reaching a verdict, a friendly query to show them you are still enthusiastic about the proposal seldom does any harm. Remember, however, that there is a fine line between being interested and being a nuisance.

FOLLOW THROUGH WHEN THE ANSWER IS "YES"

Your hard work has paid off — the answer to your proposal is "yes." This is not the time to sit back and relax, contemplating your success. You must keep up the good work.

Write a thank-you letter. If the reader is outside your organization or someone within your organization with whom you are not in day-to-day contact, promptly write a thank-you (or, at least, an acknowledgment) letter or memo. If a written message is not necessary, express your appreciation in person or over the phone.

Review the proposal. If you will be involved in executing the terms stated in the proposal, study the document before taking any action. Details that were familiar to you when you wrote the proposal may have slipped your mind during the time that has elapsed.

Keep the Acceptors Informed. If you are carrying out the proposed actions and the acceptors, for whatever reason, are removed from the situation, keep them informed of your progress. The acceptors may ask you to prepare periodic or progress reports and/or a final report, evaluating the project. If they do, you will need to keep accurate administrative and budgetary records.

FOLLOW THROUGH WHEN THE ANSWER IS "NO"

It didn't work out the way you wanted — this time. Do not put your head down on your desk and bemoan your plight. Turn the situation into a positive one by learning from it.

Express your appreciation. Although this may be the last thing you feel like doing, compose a letter or memo thanking the readers for the consideration they gave to your proposal. Remember, you want to leave the door open for future dealings. Express your disappointment but don't overdo it.

Analyze why your proposal was rejected. Forget about your ego for a while and start to look for the reasons your proposal failed. You can then benefit from what you learn the next time you write a similar proposal. In many instances you can tactfully ask the readers why they turned down your proposal. If they are willing to be candid, you can get some helpful answers from them. You may find out that outside circumstances, rather than your document's content, determined the proposal's fate. Or you may discover that your proposal was lacking in certain respects. To give you an idea of the type of questions evaluators ask themselves when considering a proposal, we have compiled a list of some of the most consequential ones:

☐ Does the proposal address one of my significant needs? Urgent needs?

☐ Does the solution overlap with what I or others are or will be doing?

☐ Is the solution cost-effective? Can someone else do it for less?

☐ Are the methods sound? Well spelled out? Is the preparer aware of possible obstacles? Are there better methods?

☐ Is the proposer qualified in terms of experience? Reputation? Credentials? Contacts? Facilities? Equipment? Financial stability?

☐ How much of a priority is this project to the preparer?

☐ Will the key personnel listed in the proposal be the people who will be put to work or are they merely window dressing?

☐ Is there a chance that the proposal will backfire once I accept it?

BE PREPARED TO NEGOTIATE

You won't always receive a gratifying "yes" or a final "no" in response to your proposal. There are times when you may, instead, meet with a noncommittal "maybe" or a "no" that is not the last word.

The readers, for instance, may be in favor of most of your proposal but also desire that you make some changes before they will consider accepting. If you agree to negotiate the terms of your proposal, keep a sharp eye out for any alterations that will compromise your or your company's integrity or interfere with your long-term goals.

Since your proposal is legally binding once accepted, any changes agreed upon by you and an outside organization should be written into the document.

THINK LONG-TERM

A judiciously prepared proposal, even if it is rejected, can put you in good stead with the readers. An improperly prepared proposal does more than dig its own grave. It creates in the readers' minds a long-lasting negative opinion of the proposer and, thus, can sabotage future opportunities.

PART THREE

Graphic Aids

Introduction to Part Three

The ability to devise graphic aids is one of the most power-
ful weapons in the arsenal of report and proposal writers.
Regrettably, most report and proposal wordsmiths do not
know how to handle that weapon to its optimum advantage.
Even if you delegate to a graphic artist the responsibility of
physically preparing the visual aids from your crude sketch,
you still must select the elements such as format and wording. After all, it is you and not the graphic artist who better
understands the readers and the points you are trying to
convey.

Graphic aids can serve your report and proposal writing
needs in one or more ways. In particular:

☐ Sometimes graphic aids are very useful, if not outright
essential, for giving your reader a clear idea of an intricate
concept or object. Imagine having to depict a complex chain
of command of a governmental bureau without an organization chart or the layout of a chemical plant without a floor
plan.

☐ Graphic aids can increase the likelihood that your report
or proposal will be read because they can provide a wel-
comed change of pace to an otherwise solid block of text.
They can also make your document more visually inviting,
a condition that is especially fruitful when reaching the
under-thirty-year-old segment of the adult population be-

cause that group was intellectually nursed by the tube. By and large, its members have a greater preference for receiving information via visual media than do the people who cut their teeth before Howdy Doody beamed his first coast-to-coast smile. The use of visual presentation in reports and proposals will increase in the future as more members of the TV generation move up the corporate ladder into policy-making positions.

☐ Often you want to make sure that the readers grasp certain facts or ideas. Graphic aids can draw special attention to important information that otherwise may be overlooked because the readers skim the text at eye-rattling speed or do not read it at all, as is the case with a typical stockholder receiving your company's annual report.

☐ If tastefully and artistically executed, graphic aids can build reader confidence. As Madison Avenue has long known, an investment in good graphic artwork can suggest that both the preparer and the document have substance.

☐ Well-chosen graphic aids, such as tables and graphs, can lend a sense of authority to a report or proposal.

☐ Graphic aids can often save space. The substance of a complex statistical table, for instance, would require far more space if the information had to be transcribed into sentence form.

☐ If well designed, graphic aids can be time-savers. They allow readers to select what is most important to them — and to see relationships and inconsistencies at a glance.

General Guidelines and Tips

☐ While it sometimes may be true that "a picture is worth a thousand words," remember that that bromide is not al ways valid. In many instances, written words by themselves are more efficient than graphic aids for communicating. Perhaps there is a no more convincing way to prove this point than to call attention to this irony: words best convey the "a picture is worth a thousand words" concept.

☐ A graphic aid, by its very nature, stands out from the text of your document as does a colorful scarf on a basic black dress. The eye, whether it is willing or not, is inexorably drawn to it. Consequently, unless you are willing to invest the time and money necessary to make a graphic aid eye-appealing and effective, you shouldn't contemplate designing it in the first place.

☐ Even if your graphic aids are capable of winning artistic awards from the Society of Illustrators, keep them to a minimum lest they eclipse the text. Some documents — such as a weekly field report from a seed salesperson — seldom if ever require them. In short, don't employ graphic aids just for their own sake.

☐ Arrange your data in the order and direction that is most familiar to your readers. If you try to be creative simply for the sake of appearing creative, you could easily forget the primary goal of your graphic aids — to communicate information. A good example of what not to do is this calendar:

	JANUARY	FEBRUARY	MARCH	
M	5 12 19 26	2 9 16 23	2 9 16 23 30	M
T	6 13 20 27	3 10 17 24	3 10 17 24 31	T
W	7 14 21 28	4 11 18 25	4 11 18 25	W
T	1 8 15 22 29	5 12 19 26	5 12 19 26	T
F	2 9 16 23 30	6 13 20 27	6 13 20 27	F
S	3 10 17 24 31	7 14 21 28	7 14 21 28	S
S	4 11 18 25	1 8 15 22	1 8 15 22 29	S

It was used in a report to the board of directors of a large American corporation. Though factually correct, it proved disconcerting to its readers. (Europeans are used to this design, but few Americans are.)

☐ "KISS" is the acronym for "Keep it simple, stupid." Eliminating all extraneous lines, words, and numbers from a graphic aid is crucial if you want to increase the chances that readers will see and digest the crux of your message.

☐ An intelligent decision on what to exclude — and what to include — in a graphic aid cannot be made unless you are aware of the readers' knowledge and limitations. If you feel it is necessary to interpret the significance of the presented information for the readers, write one or more phrases or sentences within or under the graphic aid — or, preferably, within the text of the report or proposal.

☐ You should consider rounding off numbers whenever applicable. You may, for instance, have used an electronic calculator to determine that the average weight gain of 876 female flight attendants in the first year after they were graduated from flight school was 3.923 pounds. Wouldn't the rounded figure "3.9" or even "4" pounds be easier to grasp and remember and be just as adequate for the requirements of the readers? Moreover, 3.923 is a blatant case of spurious accuracy because neither weighing methods nor scales are that precise.

☐ If you use a graphic aid, make certain that the text relates to it, but do not let the text duplicate the details of the graphic aid. If the text does not lead directly into the graphic aid, then refer to the graphic aid with a phrase on the order of:

> . . . (figure 1) . . .
> . . . see figure 2 . . .
> . . . as figure 3 indicates . . .
> . . . figure 4 shows that . . .
> . . . as suggested by figure 5, the . . .
> . . . as the adjacent figure proves . . .

If the graphic aid is on another page from the reference, you may wish to give the readers that page number.

☐ As a general rule, place the graphic aid after — but as near as possible to — the part of the text that refers to it. Size influences your decision. A small graphic aid can usually be surrounded by — or at least located on the same page as — the relevant text, while a large graphic aid typically needs to be stationed on a different page. When the latter condition occurs, that page should be the one immediately following the first reference to the graphic aid. One permitted exception: when your graphic aid takes up a full page and your document is printed on both sides of the sheet, the left-hand page may be harder to read because it does not lie flat. In this case, you may put the graphic aid on the left-hand and the reference-containing text on the right-hand page.

☐   Another exception to the "as close as possible" rule is a graphic aid that takes up more than a page because, for example, it is a lengthy table of statistics. Since such a mass of data would disrupt the flow of your text, consider placing the graphic aid in an appendix.

☐   An appendix is also ideal for a graphic aid that largely contains data that is ancillary to the text but, nevertheless, must be included for any number of reasons. If you do not, for instance, have the budget to redesign an existing published graph, you may wish to photocopy it as is and present it unedited in the appendix.

☐   Some report designers place all graphic aids in the appendix. While this technique makes the typing chore easier, it forces the readers to shuttle back and forth between the text and the graphic aids.

☐   If the text of your document is to be set in type, the layout of the pages containing graphic aids should be designed ahead of time by the trained eye of a graphic artist. A report or proposal pecked out on the typewriter, however, gives the preparer greater license in determining visual factors such as balance, though attention to fundamental mechanics such as maintaining consistent margins is still required.

☐ Resist the temptation to save space by drawing or photographically reproducing graphics too small. Readers should never have to strain their eyes.

☐ On occasion, you must reduce the size of a previously prepared graphic aid so that it can fit on the page. Again, be sure the letters and numbers can stand reduction.

☐ Another potential reduction-related problem concerns shading. If the distance between the lines of cross-hatching (or the dots of halftones such as Ben Day) is decreased too much, the wet-ink lines (or dots) may run together, creating an unattractive muddy reproduction.

☐ In the opposite vein, enlarging magnifies and therefore makes existing graphic defects all the more obvious. Over-enlarging can turn a fly speck into a distracting blot.

☐ Even if the photocopy will be the same size as the original, a hornet's nest of complications awaits the unwary duplicator. For instance, unless the original copy is clean and sharp and unless the reproduction equipment, material, and work are first-rate, the photocopy will be unworthy of a quality report or proposal.

☐ If you have the option, run the letters and numbers on the page in a horizontal (left to right) rather than in a vertical direction.

☐ If you have to rotate a graphic aid by 90° because it is too wide to place upright on a page, you have two options: you can position the top of the graphic aid next to the left-hand margin or next to the binding (see Figure 1). More than a few authorities recommend the binding method, a traditional but impractical technique. Should your graphic aid require a two-page spread (as occasionally occurs in business writing), the material would read downward on the left-hand page and upward on the right-hand page, a disconcerting change of direction. Therefore, stick with the left-hand margin method.

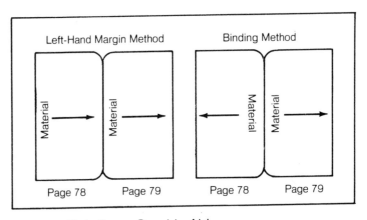

Figure 1: Rotating a Graphic Aid
by 90° to the Left or Right

☐ In most cases, a graphic aid will visually hold its position better on a page if you give it a ruled border.

☐ If your document (or a particular chapter, if your document is that involved) has only a few graphic aids, you need not number them unless specifically directed to do so. For documents with more than several graphic aids, numbering is highly advisable. Most professional report and proposal writers categorize graphic aids into two groups — tables (numbers and/or words systematically presented in columns and rows) and figures (graphs, charts, maps, illustrations, photographs, and the like). If classifying by table and figure, you would have Tables 1, 2, 3 . . . and Figures 1, 2, 3. . . .

☐ When numbering tables and figures, the Arabic system (1, 2, 3 . . .) is preferred, though, if the count is reasonably small, you may use Roman numerals (I, II, III . . .) or spelled-out numbers (one, two, three . . .). Whatever method you employ, be consistent.

☐ If your report is divided into chapters, you might choose a numbering technique that denotes both the chapter number and the table's or figure's number within the particular chapter. Thus, the fourth table in Chapter 10 would be numbered Table 10-4.

☐ Even if you number your tables and figures, you usually have the option of not numbering certain tables and figures if they are small and are placed within or adjacent to the relevant text. The calendar reprinted on page 104 and, in the sample formal report, the tables presented on pages 194 and 195 exemplify this procedure.

☐ A graphic aid requires a title unless it is small and an integral part of the text (as in the case with the calendar reprinted on page 104). Even then, a title is sometimes beneficial. A title must succinctly and accurately delineate the subject matter. Sometimes the title orients the readers by stating the gist of the conclusion or findings. A title is always positioned above a table and either above or, more commonly, below other graphic aids. Legends and other explanatory material are generally placed within or below the graphic aid.

☐ If you reproduce — or lift phraseology or findings from — a copyrighted graphic aid, secure permission from the rightful owner.

☐ As the examples that follow show, graphic aids come in all styles and shapes — and the number of subvariations is legion. It pays to acquire a working understanding of each of the basic modes because, in order to communicate your information efficaciously, you must be able to select the specific graphic aid form that best conveys your data. Rarely will two different types of graphic aids be equally suitable for your purposes. And sometimes — for optimum results — you may even have to combine the features of two or more graphic-aid designs: superimposing pictograms on the geographical areas of a map, for instance.

Bar Graphs

A bar graph consists of one or more vertical or horizontal bars superimposed on an arithmetically scaled background grid. The height or length of each bar exhibits a quantitative value for a given category. A graph's greatest virtue is that it allows the readers to see relative magnitudes at a glance.

Though there is not an ironclad rule on whether the bars should run vertically or horizontally, most designers opt for the former when measuring height, weights, percentiles, temperatures, monetary units, and physical quantities (bushels, etc.). The horizontal direction is usually selected when indicating time and length. Whatever alternative you choose, the width of the bars should be uniform and the spacing between them should be consistent.

Clearly and accurately label the bar titles, scale captions, and scale values. Use sufficient grid lines so that the readers' eyes can easily determine quantities.

Among the members of the diverse family of bar graphs, the simple bar graph is the most common (see Figure 2). It measures the quantitative value for a single set of variables such as age, time period, or geographical location.

A multiple bar chart simultaneously displays the quantitative value for two or more sets of variables (as shown in Figure 3). If you have more than three or four sets of variables in a multiple bar graph, you run the risk of confusing the readers. One solution is to combine one or more of the variables, perhaps into a "miscellaneous" or "other" cate-

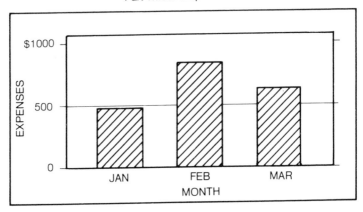

Figure 2: Simple Bar Graph

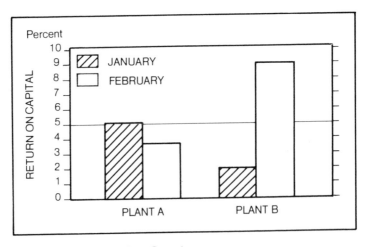

Figure 3: Multiple Bar Graph

gory. Another approach is to use two graphs rather than just one to do the job.

One usually distinguishes the sets of variables in a multiple bar graph with color or shading such as cross-hatching and/or Ben Day. An accompanying legend deciphers the graphic code. If you want to call special attention to one of the sets of variables, assign that category's bar the most conspicuous color, shading, or pattern.

A subdivided bar graph (see Figure 4) contains one or

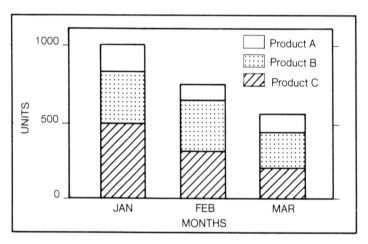

Figure 4: Subdivided Bar Graph

more bars that are partitioned into components. The full height or length of the bar is the sum (expressed in total units or as 100 percent) of those individual components. The number of components within each bar can number two or more, though more than four or five sometimes befuddles the reader. As with multiple bar graphs, graphic codes such as cross-hatching and an accompanying legend are used to distinguish one category from another. To prevent the bar from looking top- or limb-heavy, the darkest- or heaviest-looking code is assigned to the bottom component of a vertical bar and to the left-hand component of a horizontal bar. Also, one usually places the largest component at the bar's base or left-hand side.

Multiple and subdivided bar graphs are not mutually exclusive. Before concocting a multiple-subdivided bar graph, however, explore simpler approaches that would restrict the number of variables being compared so that you can comfortably stay within the realistic comprehension capacity of your average reader.

A plus-or-minus deviation bar graph is an excellent device for exhibiting changes in percentages or in fluctuating quantities such as inventories (see Figure 5). The zero-refer-

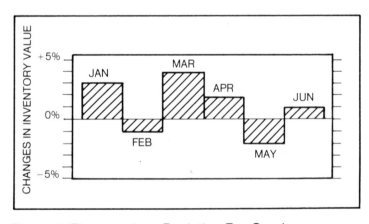

Figure 5: Plus-or-minus Deviation Bar Graph

ence line typically runs horizontally and the positive nu-
merical values are deposited above and the negative ones
below it. If you elect to position the zero-reference line vertically, align the positive values to the right side of that
perpendicular.

For the sake of reader comprehension, the scale of a bar
graph must start at a value of zero. If the magnitudes being
compared are relatively high in value and the difference(s)
between those magnitudes is relatively slight, you can save
space and emphasize differences by truncating the bars. To
truncate, you shorten the overall height or length of every
bar by removing from each an equal-sized segment. This
graphic surgery is performed somewhere above the zero

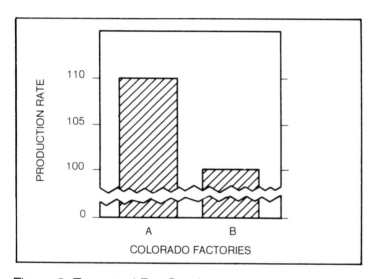

Figure 6: Truncated Bar Graph

mark and below the value of the bar with the lowest magnitude.

A truncated bar graph has one potential drawback: the hurried reader who views the bars but does not read the scale values may walk away with a misperception of the relative difference between the compared magnitudes. In Figure 6, for example, the production rate of Factory A is 10 percent — not 200 percent — greater than that of Factory B even though the bar itself rises to thrice the height of B's.

Line Charts

The line chart is the most common form of graphic aid used in business because it is widely understood and is relatively easy and inexpensive to prepare. A line chart is superior to a bar graph when you are exhibiting a trend or an ongoing series of changes that occur over small-scaled intervals. The line chart that displays the periodic fluctuations in the cost-of-living index is one of the classic examples of this breed of graphic aid.

Time customarily is charted on the horizontal (X)-axis while quantitative measurements such as monetary units are plotted on the vertical (Y)-axis. Common sense usually will tell you which axis is best for which variable.

As with a bar graph, the captions, legends, and scale values of a line chart must be clearly and accurately noted and the grid lines must be sufficient in number to allow the eye to determine quickly any plotted value.

Diligently select your scale because the casual reader's visual interpretation of the data presented in a line chart is largely based on the scale you select. Note at first glance how much more dramatic the rising prices seem to be on the right-hand as opposed to the left-hand line chart in Figure 7. Both present the same data (the prices were, for instance, five dollars in 1978 and four dollars in 1979); only the choice of scales differs. In the left-hand chart, the price scale runs from zero to one hundred dollars, while in the right-hand chart, it covers only a zero to ten-dollar range. More-

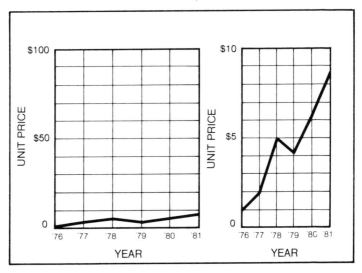

Figure 7: Effect Caused by Changes in Scales

over, the left-hand horizontal scale that is used to plot the coordinate for each year is less compressed than its counterpart.

A multiple-line chart simultaneously features two or more plotted lines on a single grid (see Figure 8). It is an excellent graphic vehicle to use when you want to compare one trend or series of values with another. Use color or design (dots, dashes, etc.) variations along with a suitable legend to help readers distinguish one line from another.

Related to the multiple-bar chart is the subdivided- or component-line chart (see Figure 9). The upper or horizon line gives the total of the components, which can be two or more, distinguished from one another with color or pattern

Line Charts

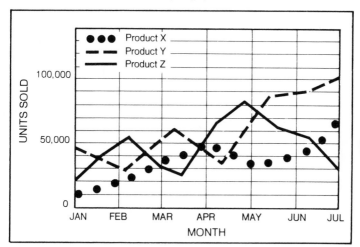

Figure 8: Multiple-line Chart

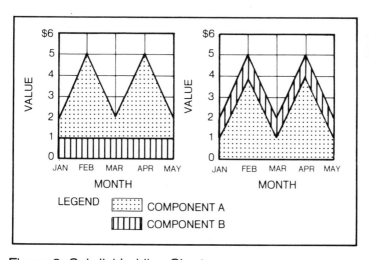

Figure 9: Subdivided-line Charts

coding. The height of each component is determined not only by its own magnitude but also by all the components laid down below it. In other words, the chart is constructed upward from the base, each added component being stacked upon the previous one. To calculate the magnitude of a component, you must subtract from the value of that component's top line the value of the top line of the component directly underneath it. (If the component is the bottom one, you need not subtract at all). Thus, the February value for Component A in Figure 9 is four dollars, while that of Component B is one dollar.

For the sake of artistically balancing a subdivided-line chart, you usually place the components with the greatest magnitude at the bottom and those with the least on top. An exception is when such an arrangement would visually distort the casual reader's perception of the data. Study the two subdivided-line charts in Figure 9. Even though Component A is larger than Component B, it should be placed above Component B (as depicted in the left-hand chart). If it is not (as illustrated in the right-hand chart), readers might gain the erroneous impression that the magnitude of Component B fluctuates.

Pictograms

One of the most effective of graphic aids is the pictogram, a highly simplified visual representation of objects or qualities such as people, houses, barrels, dollars, and productivity. These symbols can be used in conjunction with other basic forms of graphic aids including the bar graph. Pie charts and maps are other popular repositories for the pictogram.

A pictogram is a choice communication vehicle only if the selected graphic symbol quickly and unmistakably conjures up in the readers' minds the subject being depicted. Sadly, many a pictogram has scored low marks in that department.

Another potential flaw to avoid when using pictograms concerns choice of scale. Do not, for example, show an increase of 100 percent by doubling the height of your chosen symbol. When you double the height of a two-dimensional figure, you quadruple rather than double its total area and, therefore, may lead some readers to believe the increase is greater than it actually is. A case in point is Square A depicted in Figure 10. When its height is doubled, its two dimensional surface area is magnified by four times.

Even if you increase the area of a symbol in true proportion to the actual increase, your readers may discern a relationship other than the one you are trying to convey. For example, some of the hurried readers who view Figure 11 may think that the physical size rather than the population of dairy cows increased over the fifty-year time span. A better approach is to show the increase by increasing the number of symbols (in whole and/or fractional form).

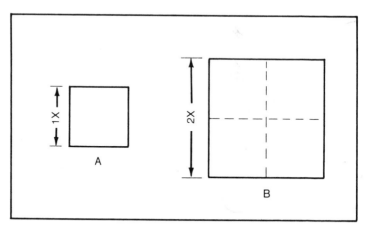

Figure 10: Effect of Doubling the Height of a Pictogram

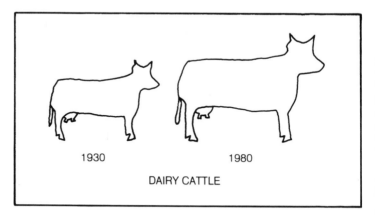

Figure 11: Pictogram Misuse

Pie Charts

A pie chart is similar to a subdivided-graph or -line chart because the whole equals the sum of the individual components. Each component is a wedge, a slice of the total pie. This form of graphic aid is easy to design and understand and is especially suited to depicting percentages (see Figure 12).

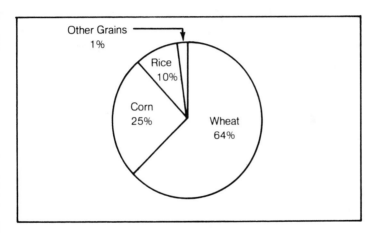

Figure 12: Pie Chart

As with bar graphs and line charts, components can be distinguished by different colors, shading and/or patterns — with each code identified in an accompanying legend. Alternatively, you can label each wedge if it is large enough to accommodate clear lettering. In order that the readers do not have to guess what percentage or part of the whole each component represents, you should include the appropriate percentage figure or value within the wedges themselves. Sometimes, however, your pie chart will contain extremely small slices. In those cases, place the caption and figure directly outside their corresponding wedge and draw an arrow from the descriptive material to the slice.

Standard procedure is to start cutting the pie at high noon — that is, at the 12 o'clock position. You then continue in a clockwise direction. Begin with the largest value and work your way around to the smallest. For the sake of visual clarity, if you have several tiny values, say 1 or 2 percent each, consider combining them into one wedge and assigning them a tag such as "Miscellaneous" or "Other." You can provide a breakdown of the category's subunits in a caption underneath the circle.

Never use two pie charts to compare two unequal wholes. Few readers can accurately perceive the relative difference between the areas of two unequal-sized circles.

Flow Charts

A flow chart is often your best choice of medium when you want to explain the interrelationships of steps in a process, such as the circuitous route of a claim report as it slowly wends its way through the home office of an insurance company or the path of a product such as an evolving television set as it travels through the labyrinthine assembly line at a plant. You will find that the flow chart usually helps your reader comprehend step-by-step activity more quickly and effectively than does expository text by itself.

The basic flow chart typically comprises a set of boxes (or other geometric forms) connected by arrows denoting the direction of flow (see Figure 13).

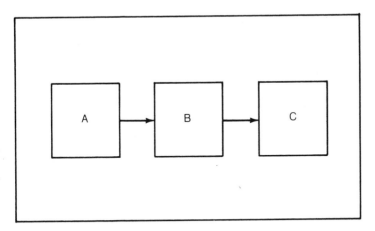

Figure 13: Basic Flow Chart

A variation of the above flow chart is the branch flow chart (see Figure 14). As its name suggests, it displays ramifications, which may or may not subsequently merge.

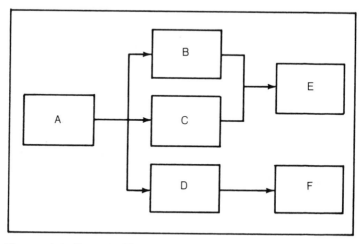

Figure 14: Branch Flow Chart

Unless you have a special reason for not doing so, indicate the flow from left to right. If you prematurely reach the right-hand margin of your paper, continue the flow on the next lower level, in much the same manner as you do when writing lines in a paragraph. One permitted exception to the left-to-right rule is in graphically illustrating a computer program. By convention, those charts proceed downward. Another exception is a circular flow chart (see Figure 15), which is used to illustrate a cyclical process such as the four seasons.

Space permitting, place the identifying captions of each

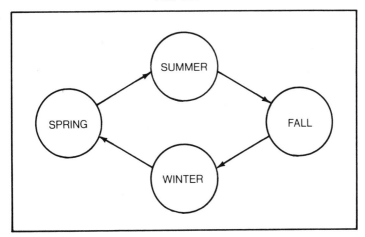

Figure 15: Circular Flow Chart

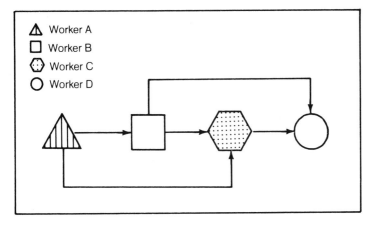

Figure 16: Symbol Flow Chart

component of a flow chart within the individual ruled boxes. If you must save space, consider using symbols such as miniature triangles and circles (with an accompanying legend) instead of caption-identified boxes. See Figure 16.

Organization Charts

A cousin of the flow chart is the organization chart. It exhibits the lines of command and/or staff relationships among individuals or offices within an organization. (See Figure 17.)

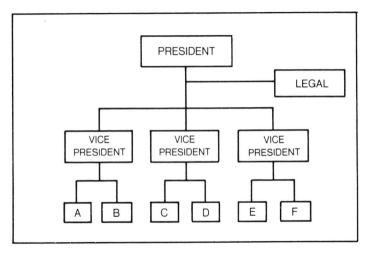

Figure 17: Organization Chart

Certain well-established procedures should be followed when constructing an organization chart. Always begin with the highest-ranking box and then design the chart downward. Any given job or office is either line (command) or staff in nature. "Vice President of Manufacturing" is an example of the first, and "Special Assistant to the President" is of the second type. If the function is line, its box is connected to its superior box with a straight or zigzag vertical line. If the function is one of staff, its box is linked into the appropriate place on the organization chart with a horizontal line.

Maps and Illustrations

A map is usually a sound choice for demonstrating geographical differences or relationships such as directions, distances, distribution, or profiles. The quantity or quality within each geographical subarea can be represented by such graphic means as shading or pattern, pictograms or other visual symbols. Identifying captions and/or the actual number count can also be incorporated within the subareas if space allows.

A sketch or line drawing can give your report or proposal visual warmth and an inviting tone — that is, if both the original artwork and the reproduction of the ready-for-camera material meet high standards. Both the sketch and line drawing have at least two key advantages over a photograph. They are less likely to suffer from poor reproduction and they better allow you to focus the readers' eyes on the specifics that you wish to emphasize. A comparable photograph, on the other hand, generally costs less and/or can give you the lifelike quality that may be necessary for your particular topic.

Tables

Last but not least among the graphic aids discussed in this book is the old workhorse, the table. A table is a graphic aid, to be sure, but it is literally the least graphic of all. It requires no special artistic talent to design save for an ability to draw a few straight lines. What gives a table its graphic nature and therefore offers a visual change of pace to an otherwise solid block of text in your document is the orderly arrangement of words and/or numbers in columns (vertical) and rows (horizontal).

PETROLEX CORPORATION SHAREHOLDERS

| | COMMON STOCK | | | |
| | Shares | | Shareholders | |
	No.	%	No.	%
Male	932,451	13.67	3,893	29.64
Female	753,466	11.04	4,036	30.73
Joint Accounts	418,712	6.14	3,143	23.93
Corporations	1.517,405	22.28	683	5.20
Brokers	39,403	.58	18	.14
Nominees	2,887,574	42.31	222	1.69
Trusts	234,564	3.44	1,102	8.39
Banks & Trust Companies	3,000	.04	2	.02
Institutions and Insurance Companies ..	39,603	.50	34	.26
TOTAL	6,820,624	100.00	13,133	100.00

Figure 18: Table

Each table should have a descriptive title and, if two or more columns are displayed, delineating captions over each column. If it serves the readers, use subcaptions as well, as is done in Figure 18.

Stubs may identify the rows and, if used, are situated immediately to the left of each row as they are in the accompanying sample table. Should the rows be particularly long, consider duplicating the stub to the right of its proper line.

PART
FOUR

Common
English
Errors

Introduction to Part Four

No matter how convincing your arguments or facts are, your report or proposal will suffer if faulty writing flaws it.

For that reason we have compiled more than seventy examples of the most common errors in English committed by business-report and proposal writers. We have divided the entries into five categories for easy reference:

> Grammar and usage in general
> Agreement between noun and verb
> Ambiguity and redundancy
> Punctuation
> Numbers and capital letters

This section is designed to be a self-teaching exercise. Each sentence on the left side of the page contains one or, in a few cases, two or three errors. We give a corrected version, along with an explanation, on the right side of the page. Cover the right side of the page, read the original sentence, and make your own change(s). Then compare your draft with our revised sentence. In some instances, it may be possible for your solution to differ from ours yet be just as acceptable. After all, even noted grammarians are not in complete agreement as to what is correct English—and our decrees merely reflect a consensus of leading contemporary authorities.

Grammar and Usage in General

They promised to promptly respond.

They promised to respond promptly.

Try not to split infinitives. Exceptions: when clarity or flow is impaired (thus, "He needs to fully comprehend the consequences" a split infinitive that is permitted).

They had, I believe, promised delivery.

They had promised delivery, I believe.

Avoid splitting multi-word verbs unless doing so is essential for clarity or flow. Example: "They were hardly listening."

They slaughtered the sheep who were ill.

They slaughtered the sheep that were ill.

Generally, use "who" only when referring to human beings. Or recast the sentence: "They slaughtered the ill animals."

Louis Pasteur discovered that heat killed bacteria.

Louis Pasteur discovered that heat kills bacteria.

COMMON ERRORS	CORRECTED VERSIONS

State universal or general truths in the present tense. The same is true when using the historical present. Example: "Thomas Edison is the father of the light bulb."

The reason the strike occurred is because he wanted it.	The reason the strike occurred is that he wanted it. [Or: "The strike occurred because he wanted it."]

"The reason is because" is grammatically incorrect.

The staff was overwhelmed, underpaid, and lacked motivation.	The staff was overwhelmed, underpaid, and unmotivated.

A string of adjectives (or nouns) that appear in a sentence should be written in parallel grammatical form. Parallel construction is one of the hallmarks of a good writing style.

They are not sure if Jones is there.	They are not sure whether [or that] Jones is there.

To use "if" correctly, it must involve a condition. [Example: "They will not act if Jones is there."]

COMMON ERRORS	CORRECTED VERSIONS

He can go no farther in this company.

He can go no further in this company.

Unless the distance is measurable ("four feet," for example), use "further."

They are angry at us.

They are angry with us.

People become angry with people, angry at situations.

Smith is the least experienced of the two candidates.

Smith is the less experienced of the two candidates.

Use "less," "faster," "better," etc. when comparing two (and "least," "fastest" and "best," etc. when comparing three or more) entities or concepts.

We plan to talk to him during the negotiation.

We plan to talk with him during the negotiation.

"Talk to" suggests one-way conversation, as in a public address.

Due to technical difficulties, the show was postponed.

Because of technical difficulties, the show was postponed.

COMMON ERRORS   CORRECTED VERSIONS

If you can directly substitute the words "because of" for "due to," then do not use the latter phrase.

The manager felt badly.   The manager felt bad.

"Bad" modifies the noun "manager" and not the verb "to feel" and is thus an adjective rather than an adverb. Note: If the manager were wearing thick gloves, then he would "feel badly."

Among Smith, Jones, and   Among Smith, Jones, and
Roberts, the former is quali-   Roberts, the first person is
fied.   qualified.

Do not use "former" (or "latter") when referring to more than two entities or concepts.

The most complete book.   The only complete book.
                                 [Or, if it is not complete:
                                 "The more (or less) nearly
                                 complete book."]

"Complete" (as well as other words such as "perfect," "circle," "final," "outstanding," "essential," "unique," "vital," "parallel," and "alive") are absolutes.

COMMON ERRORS	*CORRECTED VERSIONS*
He will sell it, providing we meet his price.	He will sell it, provided we meet his price.

"Provided" is correct when the word is used in place of "if."

If the economy improves, we may invest.	If the economy improves, we might invest.

If the occurrence of a future event is dependent upon another event, use "might." If not, use "may" ("We may invest").

The law will effect the employees.	The law will affect the employees.

When the verb means "to influence," always use "affect." When the verb means "to cause" or "to execute," always use "effect." When the word is used as a noun, always use "effect."

Over 1,000 stockholders voted.	More than 1,000 stockholders voted.

Use "more than" when referring to a number.

First, sign the contract; secondly, hire the staff.	First, sign the contract; second, hire the staff.

COMMON ERRORS   *CORRECTED VERSIONS*

Once you have written the word "first," use "second" (and so on) rather than "secondly."

Acme divides its profits between its stockholders.	Acme divides its profits among its stockholders.

Use "between" for two and "among" for three or more persons or things.

The engine broke down continuously.	The engine broke down continually.

Use "continuously" if there is no break in the action and "continually" if there is.

The engine uses less watts.	The engine uses fewer watts.

Use "fewer" when specific numbers are stated or implied. Thus: fewer watts/less wattage.

Smith graduated from Tulane University.	Smith was graduated from Tulane University.

The institution, not the student, did the graduating.

It is alright to be enthused even if you can not win.	It is all right to be enthusiastic even if you cannot win.

COMMON ERRORS   CORRECTED VERSIONS

"Alright" is not a word. "Enthused" and "can not" are not considered good English.

They go slow.   They go slowly.

A highway department can be forgiven for its grammatically incorrect "go slow" signs because the error increases reading speed and reduces space requirements. We cannot be forgiven as "slowly" is an adverb modifying the verb "go."

Hopefully, I can meet the   I hope I can meet the dead-
deadline.   line.

Since "hopefully" is an adverb, it modifies the verb "meet." Consequently, the first sentence implies that the person will meet the deadline in a hopeful state of mind. The revised sentence indicates that the person wishes to meet the deadline but is unsure about accomplishing the goal.

They could of replied ear-   They could have replied earlier.   lier.

Never use "of" when "have" works.

Neither he or she agreed.   Neither he nor she agreed.

COMMON ERRORS	CORRECTED VERSIONS
	When you use "neither" in a correlative conjunction, you must use "nor."
We will move to either Chicago, New York, or Los Angeles.	We will move to Chicago, New York, or Los Angeles.
	Do not use "either" or "neither" if more than two nouns are involved.

Agreement Between Noun and Verb

COMMON ERRORS	CORRECTED VERSIONS
Profit and loss are important.	Profit and loss is important.

Use a singular verb for a collective concept.

COMMON ERRORS	CORRECTED VERSIONS
The top management are responding.	The top management is responding.

Collective nouns generally require a singular verb. However, when you are referring to individual parts of the noun as opposed to the noun as a whole unit, the plural verb is correct. (Example: "The top management are fighting among themselves.")

COMMON ERRORS	CORRECTED VERSIONS
The economics are questionable.	The economics is questionable.

Some plural nouns always or generally require a singular verb. They are plural in form, singular in concept. Besides "economics" these words include: "acoustics," "aeronautics," "civics," "dynamics," "esthetics," "ethics,"

COMMON ERRORS · *CORRECTED VERSIONS*

"hydraulics," "linguistics," "mathematics," "means," "optics," "phonetics," "physics," "politics," "statistics," "tactics."

The memoranda has been typed.	The memoranda have been typed. [Or: "The memorandum has been typed."]

"Memoranda" is always plural. However, note that nowadays the plural noun "data" can be used as a singular noun in place of "datum."

Every employee has their grievance.	Every employee has his/her grievance.

Since the antecedent ("employee") is singular, the pronoun must be singular too.

A carton of bolts are arriving this week.	A carton of bolts is arriving this week.

A verb must agree in number with its subject. In this instance, the singular "carton," not the plural "bolts," is the subject.

Smith, along with Jones and Roberts, are attending the meeting.	Smith, along with Jones and Roberts, is attending the meeting.

COMMON ERRORS   *CORRECTED VERSIONS*

A parenthetical expression such as "along with Jones and Roberts" does not change the fact that "Smith" is the subject. Therefore, the sentence requires a singular verb.

Either the vice presidents or the president are quitting.

Either the vice presidents or the president is quitting.

When using "or" or "nor," the verb should agree in number with the latter subject. In our sample sentence, you should use the plural verb if you reverse the sequence of the subjects: "Either the president or the vice presidents are quitting."

General Motors is introducing a new car. They foresee no problems.

General Motors is introducing a new car. It foresees no problems.

Because General Motors (as well as other company names) is a singular noun, use the singular pronoun.

Ambiguity and Redundancy

COMMON ERRORS	CORRECTED VERSIONS
The press release that was distributed quickly made headlines.	The quickly distributed press release made headlines. [Or, if the other meaning is intended: The distributed press release quickly made headlines.]

When a misplaced word can modify the preceding and following words, the sentence can have two meanings. This error is called "squinting."

He only listens to her.	He listens only to her.

The first sentence suggests that he does not talk to her. Place the modifier "only" directly in front of the word or words it modifies.

When typing, the telephone rang.	When I was typing, the telephone rang.

The first sentence is grammatically incorrect unless your telephone happens to type. "Dangling modifier" is the term for this common error.

COMMON ERRORS	*CORRECTED VERSIONS*

It was the consensus of opinion that she be promoted.

It was the consensus that she be promoted.

"Of opinion" is redundant.

I must refer back to his letter.

I must refer to his letter.

"Back" is a redundant word in this sentence.

The truck is too old for people (or "for a person") to drive.

The truck is too old to drive.

Since it is obvious that the truck does not drive itself, the phrase "for people" or "for a person" is redundant.

The entrepreneur merged the three companies into one.

The entrepreneur merged the three companies.

"Into one" is redundant in this sentence.

They will clean up the factory.

They will clean the factory.

Never add "up" when the sentence is clear without it. "They will set up the display," is permitted because "up" is necessary.

COMMON ERRORS	CORRECTED VERSIONS

We are faced with four different kinds of risks.

We are faced with four kinds of risks. [Or: "We are faced with four different risks."]

It is redundant to use "different" and "kinds of" together.

Our product is equally as good.

Our product is equally good.

"As" is unnecessary.

The basic elements of the agreement were ratified.

The elements of the agreement were ratified. [Or: "The basics of the agreement were ratified."]

Elements are basic.

That answer is my personal opinion.

That answer is my opinion.

If it is your opinion, it is obviously personal unless you happen to be distinguishing between your "personal" and "professional" opinion.

They will repeat the offer again.

They will repeat the offer.

"Again" is redundant unless you are emphasizing that they are repeating the repeating of the offer.

Punctuation

|

He said, "Mr. Smith answered "maybe" to the questions."

He said, "Mr. Smith answered 'maybe' to the questions."

Use single quotation marks for quotes within quotes.

They told the manager [who was uninformed] the story.

They told the manager (who was uninformed) the story.

Do not use brackets when parentheses do the job. Major exception: when you are demonstrating that you have inserted words within someone else's quotation. Example: "Jones said, 'Do not buy the [old] equipment.' " Brackets are also used when it is necessary for the writer to make it clear that an interjected word or phrase is an editorial aside and not an inherent part of the sentence.

The 1980s will be challenging.

The 1980's will be challenging.

Use an apostrophe and "s" to make plurals out of numbers and letters. Do the same when a

COMMON ERRORS	CORRECTED VERSIONS

noun has no standard plural form. (Example: "No if's or but's.")

The X.Y.Z. Corporation defaulted.	The XYZ Corporation defaulted.

Omit the periods unless you know that they are used by the organization.

She was born on June 3, 1947 in the Monroe Hospital, 3010 East Avenue, Rochester, New York, 14610 on a sunny day.	She was born on June 3, 1947, in the Monroe Hospital, 3010 East Avenue, Rochester, New York 14610, on a sunny day.

Do not omit the middle or the final comma after dates, addresses, and geographic names. Exception: "She was born in October 1975, [or, "on 3 June 1947,"] in Rochester." Exception: Do not place a comma between the state name and zip code.

He said, "No". Did she reply "Let us cancel the deal?"	He said, "No." Did she reply "Let us cancel the deal"?

Place periods and commas inside and colons and semi-colons outside quotation marks. Place question marks, exclamation points, and dashes inside or outside the quotation marks, depending on whether the punctuation mark(s) is a direct part of the quoted material.

COMMON ERRORS	CORRECTED VERSIONS

The managers's offices were painted.

The managers' offices were painted.

It is up to you whether you want to add the extra "s" to possessive singular nouns that end in "s." (Examples: "Mr. Jones' desk" or "Mr. Jones's desk.") If the "s"-ending noun is plural, do not add the extra "s" ("The Joneses' desks").

They donated money to the Children's Aid Society.

They donated money to the Childrens Aid Society.

It is permissible for an organization to eliminate a possessive apostrophe in its proper name. If in doubt, consult the organization.

Jane's and Roger's company is financially sound.

Jane and Roger's company is financially sound.

Only the final subject receives the apostrophe and "s" if the object is jointly possessed.

The *Appliances* chapter in the "Modern Electricity" book is missing.

The "Appliances" chapter in the *Modern Electricity* book is missing.

Unless used as a headline, names of books, publications, movies, and works of art are italicized (or, on a typewriter, underlined or capitalized) — and names of chapters, articles, and poems are placed within quotation marks.

Numbers and Capitals

COMMON ERRORS

CORRECTED VERSIONS

At least $106 million dollars will be needed.

At least $106 million will be needed.

The "$" sign means dollars.

Smith will receive one thousand ($1,000) dollars by tomorrow.

Smith will receive one thousand dollars ($1,000) by tomorrow.

Note that "($1,000)" is a repetition of "one thousand dollars" rather than of "one thousand."

The two figures are .63 and 1.23

The two figures are 0.63 and 1.23

A zero is added whenever a number would otherwise begin with a decimal point.

45 workers finished the job.

Forty-five workers finished the job.

Do not begin a sentence with a numeral. If the number is 100 or more, recast the sentence (for

COMMON ERRORS	CORRECTED VERSIONS

instance: "According to Smith, 145 workers finished the job").

The company has 6 offices.	The company has six offices.

Use words rather than figures to express whole numbers or fractions that are stated in one or two words (examples: three-fourths; three hundred). Alternatively, use words if the whole number or the parts of the fraction comprise only integers from zero to ten (examples: nine-tenths; $^9/_{11}$'s). Use either rule but be consistent. One exception to both rules is the use of figures to express page numbers. With chapter numbers you have a choice.

Each warehouse has six trucks and 156 workers.	Each warehouse has 6 trucks and 156 workers.

If two or more numbers are used as part of the same series and at least one of the numbers comprises three or more words, use figures for all the numbers. Please note, however, that "The six trucks are used by 156 workers" is correct because there is no series relationship.

We used approximately three fourths of the sixty five truckloads.	We used approximately three-fourths of sixty-five truckloads.

COMMON ERRORS   *CORRECTED VERSIONS*

Hyphenate fractions that are expressed in only two words. Also hyphenate the whole numbers from twenty-one to ninety-nine if they are expressed in words.

The title of the reprint is "The Management Of Time."	The title of the reprint is "The Management of Time."

Do not capitalize a word in a title unless it is the first, the last, or a major word. Minor words include short prepositions ("to," "for," etc.), conjunctions ("and," "but," etc.) and articles ("a," "an," "the").

His doctoral thesis explores the relationship between Harry S. Truman and the famous writer, E. E. Cummings.	His doctoral thesis explores the relationship between Harry S Truman and the famous writer, e. e. cummings.

Capitalize (as well as spell, punctuate, and pronounce) a person's name as he/she prefers.

PART FIVE

Other Writing Guidelines

☐ Reports or proposals penned by a committee often lack a cohesive writing style and may even end up looking like Scylla, the six-headed monster of classical mythology. Yes, do solicit ideas from an array of qualified people, but — in the end — assign one person to be the chief or only writer of your document.

☐ Ideally, the best person to scribe the document is the individual most closely involved with the completed or proposed project. If that person does not have writing proficiency, select someone else who does — even if you have to pay for the services. More than a few reports and proposals have been hamstrung by shortcomings in style and grammar.

☐ Give yourself as much lead time as possible. An early start minimizes the danger of being unable to overcome unforeseen bottlenecks; consider the consequences of not having a vital piece of information because you were not informed that the sole source was going trout fishing for three weeks in the Rockies.

☐ Ample lead time also gives you the luxury of putting your first draft out of sight for a while before you commence writing the second draft. During this hiatus, whether it is a day or week, try to refrain from sneaking a peek at even a single word. You need this breather to help you view your thoughts and phraseology with a more objective eye.

☐ The natural tendency towards procrastination that plagues even some of the most professional of writers can rob you of valuable time. If, like most people, you find your-self hunting for convenient excuses that will postpone the hour when you reach for a blank piece of writing paper, you will benefit from the wisdom behind this Chinese proverb: The longest journey begins with the first step. You must overcome inertia by getting started. Once your words begin to flow off your pen or typewriter ribbon, momentum builds and you're on your way to finishing a first draft — that is, if you have first developed an outline and done your research.

☐   When writing the first draft, don't be concerned about verbosity, misspellings, and grammar. Neither should you be alarmed if your draft is impaired by the presence of some hazy concepts or questionable logic or by the absence of a few necessary facts. You will be in a better position to correct those flaws later. Your immediate goal is to place your rough thoughts on paper so that you can develop, edit, and refine them.

☐   "Do not insult the reader's intelligence" is a sound rule. However, if you adhere to that rule too closely, you are in danger of committing an equally blatant sin: overestimating the reader's knowledge. When you are in doubt whether the reader knows an essential detail, it is best to risk insulting his/her intelligence. Reason: if you omit the detail, the reader may conclude that you did not recognize its impor-tance or, worse yet, that you were unaware of it.

☐   To minimize ambiguities, do not write to a vacuum or abstraction. As you put your thoughts down on paper, visu-alize your reader sitting across your desk, reacting to your words. Also visualize your reader at 3 A.M. in bed with your proposal or report in hand. To forestall drowsiness, your information must be of interest to the reader. Is it?

☐ Quickly and clearly link your report or proposal with the reader's interest. Until the reader perceives this match-up, you cannot expect him/her to peruse the document diligently.

☐ A reader is more interested in how a situation relates to him/her than in how it affects you. Whenever possible, make your sentences "you-oriented." Compare:

We can manufacture the machines within the time allocated to us.	Your machines will be delivered to you within the allocated time.

☐ Come to the point early. State the most convincing and/or critical point of your report or proposal up front. Unless your first paragraph or two grab the reader's interest, chances are the subject matter buried within the body of your document will be given scant attention or none. After all, few executives have the time to read thoroughly every piece of paper sitting in the "in" box.

☐ As much as possible, anticipate you reader's questions and objections. Keep in mind that a busy executive often finds it quicker and easier to spot the weaknesses as opposed to the strengths of your report or proposal.

☐ "Accentuate the positive, eliminate the negative," as the song goes. While this advice is astute, you must be candid about shortcomings if you hope to build credibility. They seem less severe when the reader hears about them from you rather than from somebody else. State shortcomings, however, in a non-apologetic tone.

☐ Be brief and to the point so long as you are not impersonal. At least some touch of warmth is needed in effective writing.

☐ Don't be afraid to write the words "I" and "we" to refer to yourself or your company. Phrases such as "this writer" and "it is advised" can create a cold, detached, and supercilious tone.

☐ Project a confident tone, but stop short of seeming boastful or overly optimistic. In the latter case, the reader may deduce that you do not have both your feet planted firmly on the ground.

☐ Rhetoric, sweeping generalizations, hyperbole, and other forms of exaggeration antagonize intelligent readers. Use a superlative (as in "We are the most qualified" or "He is respected by everyone") only when you can substantiate your claim.

☐ Avoid obvious flattery and false modesty. Compare:

Your company is so highly respected and admired in your industry that it would be an honor for an unknown firm such as ours to become your tax consultant.

We would be pleased to serve as tax consultant for your respected firm.

☐ Weave into your document any significant feedback that you received from the intended readers via meetings, telephone calls, or written correspondence during the pre-writing phase. Such inclusion not only makes your report or proposal more relevant to the readers, it also indicates that you made good use of the valuable time they gave you.

☐ The more specific the word, the more the reader learns. Compare "I will communicate with you next week" with "I will telephone you next week."

☐ Use the short, simple word except when a longer, more complicated one is more precise and descriptive for your purposes. Another exception is when you are overusing the shorter, simpler word and must inject word variety. Be sure, however, that the chosen word will be understood by your readers and not considered pompous or otherwise in bad taste. Searching for the perfect word can be painstaking at times, but the reward is usually worth the effort.

☐ Watch out for a naked "this" or "that." In our two examples, notice how the addition of the descriptive noun ("decision") lends concreteness.

Smith said no. This eliminated us from contention.	Smith said no. This [or his] decision eliminated us from contention.

☐ Be as specific as possible. "The 1200-horsepower electric engine has to be replaced" is more descriptive than "The engine has to be replaced."

☐ Adjectives are wonderful tools because they can lend excitement and evoke vivid images ("the spotless lab"). Be sure, however, that they accurately and meaningfully modify the noun as the indiscriminate use of adjectives fogs your basic message.

☐ Use concrete examples. Consider the effect of adding "in the Acme plant" to the end of this sentence: "Our product has increased productivity."

☐ Do not expect your reader to accept your statements at face value. Whenever possible, document your assertions with facts or qualified, disinterested opinions. For instance: "The USDA forecasts a sizable increase."

☐ If you have the opportunity, quantify your statements. Compare: "The USDA forecasts a 67% increase" with the example given in the preceding paragraph.

☐ Many an otherwise winning report or proposal has been enfeebled because the writer was not aware of the innuendo of a word — or because he or she didn't select the perfect word. As Mark Twain wryly observed, the difference between the best and second-best word is often the difference between lightning and a lightning bug.

☐ Use jargon sparingly and only if you are positive that all the readers will understand and accept it. Some writers forget that their reports or proposals are often reviewed by a broad variety of unseen yet influential people with disparate backgrounds. When jargon, trade lingo, technical terms, or other unfamiliar words baffle or antagonize a reader, the power of the document is needlessly sapped. If you must use a term that may not be understood by everyone, define it in layperson's language.

☐ Explanations that seem clear to the writer are often incomprehensible to readers. Reflect back to Christmases past. How many times have you unsuccessfully tried to assemble a toy that came with "simple, easy-to-follow instructions"? No doubt whoever wrote those directions was confident that any reasonably intelligent adult or child could understand the explanations. Let that yuletide plight be an object lesson to you whenever you have to explain a concept or process. Test the comprehensibility of your statements on at least one person before implanting them in your final draft.

☐ Most modern business-writing authorities consider the sentence on the left to be sexist. It is easy to recast such sentences, as our examples illustrate:

If an employee is to be promoted in that firm, he must have a sociable wife.	If an employee is to be promoted in that firm, he/she must have a sociable spouse. [Or: "If employees are to be promoted in that firm, they must have sociable spouses."]

☐ "Ize-itis" has afflicted many an executive's writing hand. A classic example is substituting "utilize" for "use." The cure for this writer's disease is to avoid suffixing words with "ize" when the original is shorter, simpler, and identical in meaning.

☐   Some business writers use the suffix "ish" with abandon ("lawyerish" and "moneyish" are examples). Forget the "ish" unless a dictionary considers the addition proper.

☐   "Businessese" is one term for the ponderous writing style favored by bureaucrats. It clouds your writing with unnecessary and pedantic words. Compare these sentences:

Pursuant to your letter of May 29, be advised that as of this date we will take into consideration your submitted request.

We will consider your May 29 request today.

☐   "Legalese" defines yet another heavy-handed writing style. The 121-word sentence on the left was part of a release form one had to sign if one wanted to rent a safe-deposit box at the Lincoln Savings Bank in New York. Compare it with the plain English version on the right:

The liability of the bank is expressly limited to the exercise of ordinary diligence and care to prevent the opening of the within-mentioned safe-deposit box during the within-mentioned term, or any extension or renewal thereof, by any person other than the lessee or his duly authorized representative and failure to exercise

Our bank is not responsible for the property in your safe-deposit box beyond the term of lease. During that term, our responsibility is limited to taking normal precautions to prevent the box from being opened by anyone except you (or persons authorized by you or by the law).

such diligence or care shall
not be inferable from any al-
leged loss, absence, or dis-
appearance of any of its
contents, nor shall the bank
be liable for permitting a co-
lessee or an attorney in fact
of the lessee to have access
to and remove the contents
of said safe-deposit box after
the lessee's death or disability and before the bank has
written knowledge of such
death or disability.

☐ Be as informal and personal as the situation allows.
Consider the difference in the conveyed feeling between
"Enclosed is. . . ." and "I am enclosing. . . ."

☐ Compare "The fact was such that one could not avoid
it" with "The fact was inescapable." Why use seven words
when one ("inescapable") will do?

☐ Compare "Our company wishes to suggest" with "Our
company suggests." "Wishes" is verbiage that costs the
reader time. Moreover, when you beat around the bush, you
reduce the impact of your statement.

☐ Avoid repetition. The exception to this rule is when you
want to summarize your main points at the beginning and/
or end of your report or proposal.

☐   Unless you are an accomplished writer, try to keep all your sentence structures simple and short. Complex or awkward sentence structures can slow down or even impede reader comprehension. Note the difference between these two examples:

When the machine works, production increases and the owners beam because they enjoy the increased profits which help pay the mortgages on their yachts.	When the machine works, production increases. The owners beam because they enjoy the increased profits which help to pay the mortgages on their yachts.

☐   Sentences generally read more smoothly and rhythmically when you position a series of adjectives or adverbs according to their length. Read aloud and compare: "The tool is indispensable, efficient, and solid," with "The tool is solid, efficient, and indispensable." Exception: when there is a chronological sequence as in "He was investigated, arrested, and tried."

☐   The active voice ("Jones hired Smith") is more emphatic than the passive voice ("Smith was hired by Jones").

☐   Whenever possible, write in one tense. In most cases, the present tense is the easiest and most effective.

☐   The overuse of underlines and exclamation points is the writer's equivalent to "crying wolf." Most good writers let their words do the emphasizing. Compare:

We *must* do *everything* by *tomorrow!* Our deadline is *near!*	We must do everything by tomorrow. Our deadline is near.

☐ Once your final draft is in hand, get someone to scrutinize it for possible shortcomings such as factual errors, misjudgments, or blind spots. This person should be impartial, familiar with the subject matter, and willing and able to offer constructive criticism.

PART
SIX

Sources of
Information

BRITANNICA BOOK OF ENGLISH USAGE
Edited by Christine Timmons and Frank Gibney
Doubleday & Company, Garden City, New York, 1980

Among the widely sold guides of this ilk, the 655-page hard-cover *Britannica Book of English Usage* ($17.95) is one of the most comprehensive. Besides covering the subject of grammar in depth, the book serves as a reference source for foreign words and phrases, abbreviations, figures of speech, and literary allusions.

BUSINESS COMMUNICATION: A PROBLEM-SOLVING APPROACH
by Roy W. Poe and Rosemary T. Fruehling
Gregg Division, McGraw-Hill Book Company, New York, 1978

The authors use a modified case-history method to teach the reader the principles of business communications. Forty-four pages of this 308-page hardcover book ($14.80) directly focus on report writing. To help the reader gain informal report expertise, the authors state an assignment, give background information, offer sample solutions, and analyze their strengths and weaknesses. Formal reports are handled in a slightly different manner. First, the assignment is set forth and the background information provided. Then, a discussion and examples of the formal report's components are presented. Exercises at the end of the report-writing chapter also help the reader sharpen his or her writing skills.

BUSINESS RESEARCH AND REPORT WRITING
by Robert L. Shurter, et al.
McGraw-Hill Book Company, New York, 1965

Designed specifically for the report writer, this 204-page paperback ($3.95) explains many of the pitfalls to avoid during the researching and writing steps. Representative chapters include "The Purpose of a Report," "Research Methods," and "Graphic Presentation."

THE CRAFT OF WRITING
by Thomas Elliott Berry
McGraw-Hill Book Company, New York, 1974

If you want a book to peruse for suggestions on how to refine your writing, this 196-page paperback ($3.95) is one of your better choices. Examples taken from famous works of literature and from distinguished periodicals illustrate the elegance and clarity of strong writing.

DEVELOPING SKILLS IN PROPOSAL WRITING
by Mary Hall
Continuing Education Publications, Portland, Oregon, 1977

Hall has, in effect, expanded on David R. Krathwohl's book, *How to Prepare A Research Proposal* (see). Indeed, she seems to have freely borrowed from some of his work — or at least from the same original sources. Her 339-page oversized softcover volume ($10.00) is nevertheless extremely valuable because it covers the subject of proposal writing much more broadly and deeply than does Krathwohl's. As does Krathwohl, Mary Hall writes primarily for the grant-seeking audience and knows how to design a book that teaches with ease.

EFFECTIVE BUSINESS COMMUNICATIONS
by Herta A. Murphy and Chares E. Peck
McGraw-Hill Book Company, New York, 1976

Over one-sixth of this 701-page hardcover text ($18.50) is devoted to report writing. The authors discuss that subject in three chapters: "The What and How of Business Reports," "Short Reports," and "The Formal Report." Sample reports as well as learning exercises are provided.

EFFECTIVE RESEARCH AND REPORT WRITING IN GOVERNMENT
by Jud Monroe
McGraw-Hill Book Company, New York, 1980

If your purview is the government arena, you may want to invest in this 320-page hardcover volume ($15.95). *Effective Research and Report Writing in Government* even gives pointers on successfully trekking through bureaucratic mazes.

THE ELEMENTS OF STYLE, THIRD EDITION
by Willard Strunk, Jr. (revised by E. B. White)
Macmillan Company, New York, 1979

All but the most accomplished writer can gain much from this 85-page classic ($5.95 hardcover, $1.95 softcover) that has been praised by English professors and noted authors alike. Pick up a copy.

EXECUTIVE'S GUIDE TO EFFECTIVE LETTERS AND REPORTS
by William M. Parr
Parker Publishing Company, West Nyack, New York, 1976

Many of the 222 pages in the hardcover *Executive's Guide* ($12.95) are devoted to letter writing. However, the reader will find the three chapters on report writing well organized and instructive. Tips and directions are short and to the point. Key information can be grasped quickly because the author indents and numbers his main points. Although not mentioned in the title, proposal writing is briefly treated in the final chapter. Preparation of unsolicited proposals is divided into twenty easy steps.

HARBRACE COLLEGE HANDBOOK
by John C. Hodges and Mary E. Whitten
Harcourt Brace Jovanovich, New York, 1977

If your library has space for only one quick-reference grammar and punctuation guide, the *Harbrace College Handbook* should probably be the book. Its greatest strengths are its organization and index that allow you to find the correct answer with minimum fuss whenever you are in doubt about a certain rule. Since this 480-page, small-sized hardcover volume ($8.50) is as comprehensive as one could reasonably expect, few of your queries should go unanswered. *Harbrace College Handbook* is also a good self-instructing vehicle: at the end of each section are well-chosen exercises.

HOW TO LIE WITH STATISTICS
by Darrell Huff
W. W. Norton & Company, New York, 1954

A book that explores the misuses of statistics need not be boring, as this volume bears out. Huff keeps the budding statistician entertained with his glib, gutsy style without once becoming academic or esoteric. Cartoons also make the book more appealing to the large number of people who have an inborn dread of statistics. The title of this 142-page paperback ($7.95) is clever but misleading. Rather than turning you into a Machiavellian statistician, *How to Lie With Statistics* will teach you how to detect deceptions perpetrated by those number manipulators.

HOW TO PREPARE A RESEARCH PROPOSAL
by David R. Krathwohl
Syracuse University Bookstore, Syracuse, New York, 1977

Time has proven this book to be a classic among academicians who prepare research proposals. Krathwohl's updated edition — a 112-page softcover book ($2.95) — guides you through the various steps of organizing and writing a formal research proposal. For the average proposal-writing executive, the volume may be geared too much to the needs of grant seekers.

HOW TO WRITE A REPORT YOUR BOSS WILL READ AND REMEMBER
by Raymond V. Lesikar
Dow Jones-Irwin, Homewood, Illinois, 1974

The text of this 216-page hardcover book ($10.50) is as straightforward as its title. Lesikar leads the reader step by step through report writing. He logically breaks down the procedures in planning, research:ng, writing, and laying out reports. An appendix provides samples of a formal, a memo, and a letter report. One of the book's most valuable chapters gives pointers on choosing and designing graphic aids.

HOW TO WRITE REPORTS, PAPERS, THESES, ARTICLES
by John P. Riebel
Arco Publishing Company, New York, 1978

Contrary to what its title suggests, this oversized paperback ($6.00) addresses itself more to helping the reader improve his or her grammar, punctuation, and vocabulary skills. In those departments the book does a good job. The author gives numerous examples of ambiguous, choppy, and awkward writing and then rewrites each one for the reader's enlightenment. He also presents at-a-glance charts showing the exact function of the different parts of speech. The book delves into the subject of report writing, more in the appendix than in the body of the text. That appendix should prove especially useful to engineers.

THE MOST COMMON MISTAKES IN ENGLISH USAGE
by Thomas Elliott Berry
McGraw-Hill Book Company, New York, 1971

Writing that contains errors in word usage and punctuation is not only awkward, it is confusing to read. The business writer who has this 146-page paperback ($2.95) on hand has little reason to make such errors. The volume's organization and index make finding the desired information easy. You will find this reference work a good backup to the *Harbrace College Handbook* (see).

THE PROPOSAL WRITER'S SWIPE FILE II
Edited by Jean Brodsky
Taft Products, Washington, D.C., 1976

Though all fourteen sample proposals in this 136-page paperback ($9.95) are designed to obtain grants, they do illustrate various proposal-writing approaches that might give you a few new ideas on phraseology. *Swipe File II* is not a priority purchase for most business-proposal writers, but if you already have an extensive proposal-writing library and want to add to it, this book might be for you.

REPORT WRITING FOR MANAGEMENT
by William J. Gallagher
Addison-Wesley Publishing Company, Reading, Massachusetts, 1969

Gallagher does a good job of instructing his readers in the ways of report writing, but he may be a little wordy for some people's taste. He does entertain, however, by sprinkling his 216-page softcover text ($6.95) with anecdotes and writing samples that are sometimes amusing.

TECHNICAL REPORT WRITING, SECOND EDITION
by James W. Souther and Myron L. White
A Wiley-Interscience Publication, John Wiley & Sons, New York, 1977

The authors use a problem-solving approach to help teach the craft of technical report writing. Scientists and engineers will gain the most from this 93-page hardcover book ($14.95).

THE WRITER'S RESOURCE GUIDE
Edited by William Brohaugh
Writer's Digest Books, Cincinnati, Ohio, 1979

If your report or proposal research entails gathering information from diverse industry, trade, professional, and government sources, this 488-page hardcover book ($11.95) will probably save you time. *The Writer's Resource Guide* gives you the name and address of the source, the type of information that is and is not obtainable, and the person to contact.

WRITING: A PRACTICAL GUIDE FOR BUSINESS AND INDUSTRY
by Charles W. Ryan
John Wiley & Sons, New York, 1974

Although you will find only two extremely brief chapters that concentrate on reports and one on proposals, you might find this book worthwhile if you also want to study guidelines that are given for business writing in general. Every chapter in this 256-page paperback ($4.95) concludes with a self-test and accompanying answers.

WRITING COMMUNICATIONS IN BUSINESS AND INDUSTRY
by Nelda R. Lawrence
Prentice-Hall, Englewood Cliffs, New Jersey, 1974

Both practical information and self-teaching work-exercises on writing reports, proposals, and letters are presented in this 167-page oversized paperback ($8.95). *Writing Communications in Business and Industry* has more than its fair share of sample reports and proposals and gives some of the basics of developing effective writing skills and format design. Representative chapters include "Using the Right Words," "Creating an Appealing Tone," and "Planning and Writing Reports and Proposals."

WRITING A TECHNICAL PAPER
by Donald H. Menzel, et al.
McGraw-Hill Book Company, New York, 1961

Scientists, engineers, and anyone who must report on scientific or engineering subjects will appreciate the tips this volume offers on how to avoid common technical-writing mistakes. All phases of preparation are covered in this 132-page paperback ($2.95).

PART
SEVEN

Sample
Reports
and
Proposals

Introduction to Part Seven

We custom-designed the reports and proposals in Part Seven for you. Rather than reprint actual business documents, we created fictitious events, people, and organizations.

If we had merely reprinted existing reports and proposals, we would have saved ourselves a lot of time and bother. We would have also shortchanged you. The chief problem with using existing business documents is they are so specialized that they would likely be boring to anyone not intimately involved with the topic. We know. Our files overflow with reports and proposals that were gathered from a wide cross-section of the business world.

There is another problem with reprinting existing reports and proposals. They are not the best teaching aids.

By writing the reports and proposals in Part Seven, we can serve you better in two ways. We can select topics that won't put you to sleep. We can give you vivid examples of how to put into the action the principles we discuss in Parts One through Five of this book. (At the end of Part Seven, there is a self-teaching exercise that will reinforce your knowledge of those principles.)

Part Seven has six sample documents:

> Sample A: Formal Report
> Sample B: Letter Report
> Sample C: Memo Report
> Sample D: Formal Proposal

Sample E: Letter Proposal
Sample F: Memo Proposal

When reading Sample A, keep in mind that we take two steps for expediency's sake. First, to save space, we do not give examples of all the ten components of a formal report that we discuss in Part One, "Report Writing." We present the four most commonly used components (title page, introduction, body, and conclusions) but not the other six components (contents, letter of authorization, abstract, appendix, bibliography, and index). We also don't present a cover letter. Second, to help you locate the subcomponent in Sample A that corresponds to our discussion in Part One, we use the same subcomponent titles that we use in Part One. In actual business situations, a more descriptive subcomponent title such as "The Problem: A Decline in Sales and Market Share" almost always would be preferable to "The Problem."

For reasons similar to the ones given in the preceding paragraph, we were also forced to exercise a bit of editorial license in "Sample D: Formal Proposal." We present only some of the components that we discuss in Part Two, "Proposal Writing," and we use the same subcomponent titles that we use in Part Two. Normally, your formal proposals would have more components and your subcomponents would have descriptive titles.

Sample A: Formal Report

A report on
SUNNYSIDE DAIRY'S
1980 MARKET DECLINE

submitted to
KRIS KRIEG
VICE PRESIDENT OF NATIONAL MARKETING
CONGLOMERATE INDUSTRIES, INC.
Chicago, Illinois

on
March 23, 1981

by
WARREN E. TOTE
RESEARCH DIRECTOR
WEST COAST DIVISION
CONGLOMERATE INDUSTRIES, INC.
San Francisco, California

INTRODUCTION AND SUMMARY

Two weeks ago you asked me to investigate why Sunnyside Dairy's market position plunged in 1980. After gathering and evaluating the evidence, I have come to this conclusion: The underlying cause of the decline was the switch by Sunnyside's two key competitors to cooperative advertising programs. I recommend that Sunnyside Dairy explore the possibility of using the same advertising strategy.

THE PROBLEM

One of our subsidiaries, Sunnyside Dairy in Metro City, lost its market position in 1980. Its supermarket milk sales for that year totaled $21,600,000, a 24-percent market share. In comparison, the 1979 sales figure was $34,200,000, a 38-percent market share.

The 1980 sales decline came after several years of steady growth. When Conglomerate Industries purchased Sunnyside Dairy in 1974, the market share was 21 percent. Sunnyside's current managerial team increased that share each year from 1975 to 1979.

THE PURPOSE OF THIS REPORT

You assigned this report to me on March 9, 1981 to 1) determine why supermarket sales of our Sunnyside Dairy milk dropped in Metro City in 1980 and 2) suggest a remedy.

SCOPE AND LIMITATIONS

My report deals only with supermarket sales because they account for 94% of Sunnyside's total revenues. My report does not cover sales to small retail stores or institutions.

My report focuses on sales for only two years: 1979 and 1980. Data for the previous years is too meager to be of much help in analyzing the problem.

DEFINITION OF TERMS

The Metro City market area comprises Metro City proper and the adjoining towns of Promville, Trager, and Goodstone.

The term "milk" as used in this report includes these products: whole milk, skim milk, and buttermilk.

"Supermarket penetration" defines the percentage of supermarkets in the Metro City market area that carry a particular milk brand.

METHODOLOGY AND SOURCES

First, I compiled the 1979 and 1980 market-share percentages for all Metro City dairies. Then I investigated those factors that could possibly cause or contribute to the drop in the market share for Sunnyside Dairy. Specifically, I looked for significant changes that might have occurred between 1979 and 1980 in:

> market penetration
> shelf position
> advertising budget
> advertising program
> sales force size
> sales force effectiveness
> product characteristics and image
> product pricing
> legislation
> unusual disruptions

To learn how shoppers as well as buyers for the supermarkets view our products and the competition's, I commissioned Market Intelligence Group, Inc. (MIG), a respected Metro City research organization. As part of the assignment, MIG also investigated where the supermarkets place the three major brands in the dairy case. Appendix A, "The MIG Surveys," details that firm's credentials and explains the methodology it used.

Data on sales volume, market share, market penetration, and advertising budgets of Sunnyside Dairy's competition was culled from recent issues of Regional Dairy Journal. The complete relevant tables published in that magazine appear in Appendix B, "Reprints from Regional Dairy Journal."

Statistics measuring the relative effectiveness of the 1979 and 1980 advertising programs were compiled by the Advertising Research Institute of America (ARIA). Appendix C, "ARIA Metro City Milk Advertising Study," presents the highlights of that inquiry.

All the quantitative data for the Sunnyside Dairy operation were supplied to me by Earl T. Coupette, the chief accountant for our Metro City subsidiary. I also interviewed the subsidiary's public relations director and sales manager. (Sunnyside's President was on vacation, backpacking in the Himalayas and could not be reached.)

THE FINDINGS

Market Share: Metro City supermarket milk sales for all dairies were $90,000,000 in both 1979 and 1980. The market-share percentages were:

MARKET SHARE

Dairy	1979	1980	Change
Sunnyside	38%	24%	− 32%
Hilltop	29%	37%	+ 28%
Woodland	29%	35%	+ 21%
Others	4%	4%	0%

Supermarket Penetration: In 1979 and 1980, the supermarket penetration figures were:

SUPERMARKET PENETRATION

Dairy	1979	1980	Change
Sunnyside	80%	69%	− 14%
Hilltop	70%	81%	+ 16%
Woodland	69%	77%	+ 12%
Others	15%	15%	0%

Shelf Position: Last week, MIG studied the shelf position that supermarkets allocated to the milk from Sunnyside, Hilltop, and Woodland Dairies. Here are the results:

SHELF POSITION DESIRABILITY

Milk	Good	Average	Poor
Sunnyside	15%	25%	60%
Hilltop	45%	40%	15%
Woodland	40%	45%	15%

According to Ron Rodriquez, sales manager for Sunnyside Dairy, the shelf position of the three brands during 1980 closely resembled the MIG findings. He also is positive that during 1979 Sunnyside milk received a better shelf position than did the Hilltop and Woodland products.

Advertising Budget: Each dairy spent $500,000 per year in advertising during both 1979 and 1980. None of the three dairies benefited from any advertising or publicity programs other than the ones they created locally.

Advertising Program: In 1979, Sunnyside, Hilltop, and Woodland each spent their entire advertising budgets on local newspaper ads that they placed themselves. In 1980, Sunnyside continued this advertising strategy. In contrast, in 1980 both Hilltop and Woodland Dairies switched entirely over to a coop advertising program with the supermarkets, which gave the supermarkets much control over how the dairies' advertising dollars would be spent.

According to Advertising Research Institute of America, the 1980 advertising programs of Sunnyside,

Hilltop, and Woodland had the same direct impact on the milk-buying public as they did in 1979. Hilltop and Woodland are expected to continue their current advertising programs.

Sales Force Size: The decrease in sales reduced the workload for the Sunnyside sales/delivery staff, so Ron Rodriquez reduced the size of that staff by 6 percent. Hilltop and Woodland, on the other hand, had to increase their sales/delivery staffs because of their expanded trade. All the buyers in the supermarkets that MIG surveyed said that these changes in staff size had no effect on the service they were receiving from Sunnyside, Hilltop, or Woodland.

Product Characteristics and Image: Ninety-five percent of the buyers for supermarkets and 90 percent of the shoppers polled by MIG do not believe that there is any difference among the three major brands of milk in terms of quality or packaging appeal and durability. Moreover, less than 10 percent of the shoppers polled are staunchly loyal to a given milk brand. Sunnyside's public relations director, Patti Lang, told me that there have been no changes in the incidence or severity of customer complaints between 1979 and 1980. She also said that none of the three major dairies received especially good or bad publicity during 1979 or 1980. Lang is convinced that milk sales are not affected by what the public thinks about

Sunnyside, Hilltop, and Woodland's other products (cream, cottage cheese, and yogurt).

Product Pricing: Retail prices for whole milk in 1979 and 1980 were, respectively, 55¢ and 59¢ for both Sunnyside and Hilltop, and 54¢ and 58¢ for Woodland Dairy.

Legislation: The only new legislation to affect the local dairy industry during the 1979 to 1980 period was the enactment of an open-dating code bill. All three major dairies implemented this dating-code system, as required by law, on February 1, 1980.

Unusual Disruptions: None of the three major dairies suffered any unusual disruptions such as a work stoppage caused by a strike.

ANALYSIS

Clearly, in 1980, Hilltop and Woodland Dairies captured a significant slice of the Metro City milk market from Sunnyside Dairy.

Because the following variables remained relatively constant for Sunnyside, Hilltop, and Woodland Dairies during 1979 and 1980, they had little or no influence on the market shift: advertising budget, sales force effectiveness, and product characteristics and image. Price increases and new legislation affected all three brands equally, and therefore can be discounted as causes for the change. There were no major disruptions at any dairy during 1979 or 1980 to account for Sunnyside's decline from number one to number three in the Metro City milk market.

Though both the market share and the size of the sales/delivery staff of Sunnyside Dairy fell while those for Hilltop and Woodland Dairies grew in 1980, the evidence indicates that the change in staff size did not precipitate the market-share shift. After all, Sunnyside's cutback in personnel was but a fraction of its drop in sales — and it was an after-the-fact response to the sales decline. Moreover, according to the supermarket survey, the augmented sales/delivery forces for Hilltop and Woodland did not give either dairy a new competitive edge.

In the milk market, as the MIG findings verify, most consumers are not loyal to a particular label. Nor does any brand have a unique sales appeal. Most milk shoppers tend to grab the brand that is most accessible. Therefore, the fact that supermarket penetration and shelf positioning worsened for Sunnyside and improved for Hilltop and Woodland did have a considerable effect on sales.

Notwithstanding, the changes in supermarket penetration and shelf positioning were not the underlying cause of the problem. The key issue is: What spurred the supermarkets into giving Sunnyside less and Hilltop and Woodland more product exposure? By matter of elimination, the only reasonable answer is that Hilltop and Woodland's switch to cooperative advertising programs pleased the supermarkets.

RECOMMENDATIONS

Sunnyside Dairy's advertising director should seriously investigate the feasibility of creating a coop advertising program with the supermarkets. And, because of the severity of the 1980 market-share loss, that investigation should begin immediately.

Sample B: Letter Report

April 2, 1981

Mrs. Grace Shuler
Executive Vice President
McCann Bakers
200 Greenwillow Avenue
Ramsey, NJ 07446

Dear Mrs. Shuler:

This morning you asked my advice on whether you should lease the GM 200X or the Ford 1000Z truck from my firm for one year. If you expect your mileage to be less than 50,000 per year, lease the GM model. Otherwise, lease the Ford model.

The only criterion I used in reaching that conclusion was the out-of-pocket cost to you because, as we agreed on the phone, both truck models should serve your purposes equally in terms of design, capacity, and dependability.

Sample B: Letter Report

My one-year lease fee is $16,000 for the GM and $17,250 for the Ford model. Based upon my past experience, you will probably have to spend about $750 in maintenance for the GM and $500 on the Ford model.

I estimate that all your other fixed costs — including insurance and permits — will run you $1,200 per year for either truck.

Based upon manufacturer's estimates for the type of driving that your operation entails, you can expect to get an average of nine miles per gallon of gas with the GM and an average of ten miles per gallon of gas with the Ford model. The American Gas Station Association estimates that the cost of the type of gas that you will be using will average $1.80 per gallon over the next twelve months.

Based upon the figures presented above, your fixed costs for the GM truck will be $1,000 less than for the Ford truck. However, you will have to pay $.02 more per mile on gas for the GM model.

I calculated the $1,000 fixed cost difference by subtracting the combined lease and maintenance costs for the GM model ($17,950) from that of the Ford model ($18,950). I calculated the $.02 difference in gas cost by subtracting the per-mile gas cost for the Ford model ($.18) from that of the GM model ($.20). I previously arrived at the $.18 and $.20 costs by dividing the cost per gallon ($1.80) by, respectively, the ten miles per gallon estimated for the Ford and the nine miles per gallon estimated for the GM truck.

Finally, I arrived at the 50,000-mile-per-year figure by simply dividing the fixed cost difference ($1,000) by the gas-cost-per-mile difference ($.02).

Please call me if you have any further questions.

Sincerely,

Maxwell Casio
Account Executive

Sample C: Memo Report

MEMO TO: Ralph Morrow   DATE: April 8, 1981
FROM: Cliff Shoenfeld
SUBJECT: OFFICE MANAGER JOB APPLICANT
                 JOHN MURPHY

Here's the report that you asked me to prepare on whether we should hire your nephew, John Murphy, as office manager.

John Murphy worked as assistant office manager at Aldora Chemical Corporation for the last three years. (I've attached his résumé.) The Aldora personnel director, Jane Fogg, told me that Murphy's general performance on the job and his ability to work with others were excellent. She said, however, that he was let go because of his habitual tardiness and absenteeism.

Murphy's only other full-time employer, Zettone Glass Works, also laid him off. His former supervisor at that firm was unwilling to tell me the specific reason for the dismissal. When asked whether he would recommend Murphy, the supervisor responded, "Sure. Everyone liked him when he worked for Zettone."

I wrote to Murphy's personal references. All three gave him glorious recommendations.

Murphy's résumé demonstrates that he is qualified for the office-manager job. My research indicates that he is good at dealing with people, an important quality for the office manager's role. On the other hand, his punctuality and attendance record suggests that he might set a bad example at our firm.

Therefore, I recommend that we do not hire Murphy for the office-manager position.

Sample D: Formal Proposal

a proposal for
RECRUITING FIFTY EAST COAST DEALERS
BY YEAR'S END

submitted to
PETER WONG
PRESIDENT
CONFUCIUS HIKING BOOT COMPANY
244 Budrow Street
Denver, Colorado 80202

on
March 24, 1981

by
WANDA FERNANDEZ
ACCOUNT SUPERVISOR
TRADE SHOW REPS, INC.
200 Park Avenue
New York, NY 10017
(212) 555-8030

INTRODUCTION AND SUMMARY

Your organization needs to sign up at least fifty East Coast sporting goods stores to carry its hiking boots. As you told me during my visit to your factory last month, this enlistment must be accomplished by the end of the year and at a cost of no more than five hundred dollars per recruit.

You should be able to recruit those dealers in time and well below your $500-per-recruit limit if you allow Trade Show Reps to execute its plan. Specifically, my firm will set up and manage a booth for you at the East Coast Sporting Goods Trade Show in New York City in December at a cost to you of $13,664.

The well-known camping authorities, Billy and Sally Richards, will be at your booth to draw people and to recommend your product. Your booth will have an excellent location if you sign and return the enclosed contract before April 10, the day when the option on the space expires.

THE NEED

Though Confucius hiking boots are widely and successfully sold in sporting goods stores west of the

Mississippi River, no sporting goods stores carry your product in the East. Your firm — if it is to remain competitive — must sign up some East Coast dealers. You specified that you need fifty dealers on the East Coast by the end of the year — and that you can afford to invest up to five hundred dollars to recruit each new dealer.

OBJECTIVE

The goal is to design and execute a plan that will get you the fifty East Coast dealers that you need — and to do so before December 31, 1981, and at a cost within your budget.

THE METHODS

There are four basic ways for you to recruit the fifty dealers: You can build and then send a sales staff to visit sporting goods stores in the East; you can work through jobbers; you can undertake an advertising and direct-mail campaign; you can reach the dealers when they attend the East Coast Sporting Goods Trade Show at the Manhattan Exhibition Hall in New York City on December 3 and 4, 1981.

Your first option — putting a sales force on the road — is cost-ineffective because the East Coast stores are spread from Maine to Florida and your potential sales volume does not justify such an expenditure.

Your second option — working through jobbers — is out of the question because you told me that your firm does not want to sell through a middleman.

Your third option — an advertising and direct-mail campaign — is impractical, according to a recent study of your industry by the independent American Business Research Organization (ABRO). That institute found that, although trade-magazine advertising and direct mail is cost-effective for most promotion purposes, it is cost-ineffective for recruiting new dealers. (See Appendix A, "ABRO Study," for the relevant portions of the study.)

Your fourth option — reaching the dealers by renting a booth at the trade show — makes sense. Most sporting goods manufacturers of your size use trade shows as their principal means of recruiting dealers.

You should be able to recruit the fifty dealers with relative ease because your product has a solid reputation and because a large share of your potential dealers will be at the East Coast Sporting Goods Trade Show. Its organizers expect that 87 percent of the East Coast sporting goods stores doing annual sales of one million dollars or more will be represented. Predicted attendance for the under-one-million-dollars-per-year stores is 52 percent. All totaled, there will be buyers from three thousand stores. And these people are coming to the show for the express purpose of buying next season's line.

You explained that your firm does not want to get involved in setting up and managing a booth because you lack the necessary experience and are too far removed from New York. We have that experience and proximity and can use those qualities in your behalf.

I realize that there is a potential problem that could arise at the trade show: light traffic to the booth caused by an undesirable booth location or by a lack of a drawing card. My plan assures heavy traffic.

Another potential problem is bad project management. What happens, for instance, if some of the supplies do not arrive in time for the show? Since I will be personally supervising this project, I do not believe you need to have any fear along this line.

Below are the key elements of my plan. (For the finer details, such as show hours, see Appendix B, "Detailed Operating Plan.")

Develop Attractions that Draw People to the Booth — Billy and Sally Richards, the husband and wife team who wrote the current best-selling book, Back to Nature, A

<u>Guide</u> <u>to</u> <u>Camping</u>, happen to be fans of your hiking boots. They have been wearing them for years. The Richards have agreed to tout your boots at the trade show for a fee plus expenses. The Richards are well known and respected among sporting goods dealers.

The secondary attraction will be a huge glass bowl of fortune cookies that contain this prophecy: "Confucius say: Stores that sell my boot will make lots of loot." The fortune strips inside twenty of the cookies will be embellished with red stars. A sign in the booth will alert passers-by that if they find a red star on their fortunes, they will receive a free autographed copy of the Richards book. My firm will arrange for a local Chinese bakery to print, bake, and deliver the needed 4,000 fortune cookies.

<u>Generate</u> <u>Pre-</u> <u>and</u> <u>Post-Show</u> <u>Publicity</u> — The New York-based publicity firm with which we work closely, Mandolay Public Relations Agency, strongly believes that it can get pre- and post-exhibit press coverage of your participation in the trade show. Mandolay plans to take photographs of Billy and Sally Richards examining the Confucius hiking boot sometime in July and another set of photographs of them at your booth during the show. (The Richards have agreed to this plan.) Mandolay will send both groups of photos to the two industry magazines. The Editor of <u>Outdoor</u> <u>Equipment</u> has already said that if the pre-event photo of the Richards

were available, he would run it with a caption in the December issue, the one that is distributed at the show. See Appendix C, "Mandolay Public Relations Campaign," for that agency's complete publicity plan.

Rent a Booth with a Prime Location — One of the best locations at the trade show is Booth Number 230/231. It is on the main exhibition floor and just in front of the principal escalator. (See Appendix D, "Trade Show Floor Plan.") Because of my long-standing relationship with the trade-show organizers, I have been able to secure an option (expires April 10) on that booth for you. If that option is allowed to expire, you will have to settle for a less desirable location.

Design an Attractive, Attention-Grabbing Booth — Reny Martino of our firm is known as one of the best booth designers in the business, and it appears she has come through for you. You will find her sketch of the Confucius Hiking Boot booth in Appendix E, "Booth Design." My firm will take full responsibility for renting the equipment and furniture (display cases, tables, chairs, backdrop curtain, rug, etc.) and for commissioning the hand-painted signs for the booth. We will also take full charge of assembling and disassembling the booth.

Adequately Staff the Booth — There is little doubt that thousands of show attendees will be visiting your booth. Consequently, the booth must be staffed with enough personnel to answer questions, hand out literature, and sign up dealers. Besides Billy and Sally Richards, four other people will be required: two of your West Coast salespersons, as well as one full-time hostess and one part-time hostess for the peak hours. These hostesses will help your sales staff pass out literature. You will be responsible for getting your salespersons to New York and for arranging their lodging and meals. My firm will hire the hostesses.

Stock the Booth with Necessary Material — On display at the booth will be two dozen pairs of Confucius hiking boots plus "Big Foot," your four-foot-long cut-away model that reveals the unique construction of your boot. The booth will also be stocked with five thousand copies of your four-color booklet that explains and illustrates why your boots are the ideal choice for hikers. You will be responsible for sending the boots, "Big Foot," and the booklets to my office. I must have them at least three working days before the show opens. My firm will be responsible for transferring them to the exhibition hall and for sending the boots, "Big Foot," and any leftover booklets back to you after the show is over.

THE QUALIFICATIONS OF TRADE SHOW REPS

For the past seven years, my firm and I have specialized in helping companies such as yours set up and operate booths at trade shows in New York City. Our clients for the upcoming East Coast Sporting Goods Trade Show are Mohawk Sleeping Bag Manufacturers and West River Freeze-Dried Foods, Inc. We have represented them at the show for the past four years. You will find the names of all our clients in Appendix F, "Trade Show Reps Client List."

EVALUATION

The project will be successful if at least fifty East Coast sporting goods stores sign up at the booth to carry your product.

BUDGET

We will bill you $13,664 (payable within ten days after the close of the trade show). That sum includes our $3,500 management fee plus the $10,164 expenses that we will pay on your behalf. Those reimbursable expenses are itemized below:

		TOTALS
PERSONNEL:		
Full-time hostess = 16 hours @ $12	$192	
Part-time hostess = 8 hours @ $12	$96	
SUBTOTAL: PERSONNEL		$288
OUTSIDE SERVICES:		
Billy and Sally Richards' fee	$2,500	

		TOTALS
Mandolay Public Relations Agency fee	$500	
SUBTOTAL: OUTSIDE SERVICES		$3,000
RENT:		
Booth Space 230	$2,400	
Booth Space 231	$1,700	
SUBTOTAL: RENT		$4,100
UTILITIES:		
Telephone installation	$37	
Telephone base rate	$50	
Telephone message units = 100 @ $.20	$20	
SUBTOTAL: UTILITIES		$107
EQUIPMENT:		
Rental of display cases, tables, and chairs	$500	
Rental of backdrop curtain, rug, and glass bowl	$225	
Rental of all other items (ash trays, etc.)	$50	
SUBTOTAL: EQUIPMENT		$775
SUPPLIES:		
Fortune cookies = 4,000 @ $.08	$320	
Stationery (pencils, paper, etc.)	$30	
Books (Back to Nature) = 20 @ $10	$200	
SUBTOTAL: SUPPLIES		$550
TRAVEL:		
Round trip Boston to New York airfare for the Richards = 2 persons @ $100	$200	
Per diem expenses for the Richards = 2 persons @ $90 per day for 2 days	$360	
SUBTOTAL: TRAVEL		$560

	TOTALS
MISCELLANEOUS EXPENSES:	
Hand-painted signs for booth	$200
Tips for Manhattan Exhibition Hall workers	$100
SUBTOTAL: MISCELLANEOUS EXPENSES	$300
GENERAL RESERVE:	
@ 5% of the overall itemized budget	$484
GRAND TOTAL:	$10,164

Your participation at the trade show will, of course, cost you more than our $13,664 billing because that figure does not include other expenses such as the cost of sending two salespersons to New York. However, the difference between your maximum budget of $25,000 (fifty recruits at $500 each) and our billing of $13,644 is $11,336. That amount will more than amply cover any costs that you will have to pay directly.

PROGRAM'S FUTURE

My firm would be more than happy to represent you at future trade shows in New York City. We enjoy working with our clients on a long-term basis.

Sample E: Letter Proposal

April 14, 1981

Mr. James Borg
President
Sparkle Soap Company
1700 Seaview Avenue
San Diego, California

Dear Jim:

During our golf game last Sunday you told me that your firm's profit margin has been steadily declining over the past five years. Obviously, the only way to stop this slippage is to raise your prices or reduce your costs. My firm, Chemcorp, can help you reduce your costs.

You disclosed to me that you are about to sign a contract with one of my competitors, Millexco Chemical Corporation, to purchase Chemical 23X17B. This one-year contract obligates you to buy 29,400 gallons at $44.86 per gallon. You will be paying $1,318,884 for the year's supply.

Chemcorp will sell the identical chemical to your company under the same one-year, 29,400-gallon conditions for only $43.97 per gallon — or $1,292,718 for the year. You'll save $26,166.

Rest assured that my firm's product is identical to Millexco's. In order not to violate and nullify the licensing agreement with the inventor of the patented Chemical 23X17B, a manufacturer must use a set formula and processing technique.

Millexco can deliver any quantity of the product to you within three days' notice. Chemcorp requires four days. Since your firm usually plans its purchases well ahead of time, I don't think one day's difference is a major factor.

Chemcorp is reliable. We have not missed a delivery deadline to any of our contract customers since we were founded in 1907.

Chemcorp is raising its prices across the board by $.50 per gallon on May 1. I can guarantee you the $43.97 per gallon rate if you sign the enclosed contract before the end of this month. Please let me know if you have any questions. I look forward to serving you.

Best regards,

John Tantoni
District Sales Manager

Sample F: Memo Proposal

MEMO TO: George Romanov   DATE: February 20, 1981
FROM: Jean Tanaka
SUBJECT: INCREASING THE NUMBER OF
                 EMPLOYEE PARKING SPACES

I am requesting authorization to spend $6,000 a year for the next five years to gain twenty-five parking spaces for our employees.

Since we expanded our labor force from 100 to 120 people last December, there haven't been sufficient parking spaces for all our employees. Unless employees drive into the parking lot at least twenty minutes before the morning's work whistle, they won't find a space. When that situation occurs, they have to search for a parking space along the street — and, sometimes, they have to park blocks away, which often causes them to be late for work. Our personnel director, Tim Kordo, has already received dozens of oral and written complaints from the workers. He also says that the percentage of workers who report late to work on an average day has increased from 2 to 5 percent in the last two months. Kordo conservatively estimates that the direct and indirect costs resulting from the space shortage will be $10,000 a year.

We can't expand our existing parking lot. To do so horizontally would require more space. We have none available. To do so vertically (building multi-layer parking) would cost roughly $5,000 per new space and, therefore, would be prohibitively expensive. Besides, the construction of such a facility would put some of our existing parking spaces out of service for months.

We do not have the option of renting spaces in a commercial parking lot or garage because the closest one is a mile away.

My assistant, Bing Simpson, has come up with a practical solution.

The empty lot across Fairmont Street has room for twenty-five parking spaces. Tim Kordo estimates that we need twenty new spaces now and will need approximately five more spaces within a year or two.

Simpson contacted the owner of the empty lot and negotiated the following arrangements. If we sign the deal before February 27, the owner will surface the lot with quality Bel-Tarmac within thirty days and then rent the lot to us at $500 per month ($6,000 per year) for a five-year contract period. (He staunchly refuses to sell the property at any price because he is "saving it for his grandchildren.")

The $6,000 annual expense works out to $240 per year per parking space. To put it another way, we will be paying $.96 per work day per new parking space. (I base that calculation on 250 working days per year.)

The expenditure is sound. Consider what the parking-space shortage is costing our company in terms of employee morale and tardiness. And the shortage is expected to become more severe.

I'll be out of town for the next three days, but if you need more information, Simpson will be around to supply it to you.

Self-Teaching Exercise

Each of the six sample documents demonstrates at least a dozen report- or proposal-writing principles, the ones we examine in Parts One through Five of this book. Try to identify as many of those principles as you can. To give you a head start, we pinpoint a few of them for you.

SAMPLE A: FORMAL REPORT

☐ Kris Krieg needs only to read the "Introduction and Summary" component to get the gist of the report. ☐ Warren E. Tote keeps Krieg from asking himself, "Why didn't Tote analyze the pre-1979 data?" with the final sentence in the "Scope and Limitations" component. ☐ Tote's conclusions are a logical outgrowth of the findings. If he had written a fact-giving report and, therefore, had not provided an analysis and recommendations, Krieg probably would have come up with the same conclusions Tote did.

SAMPLE B: LETTER REPORT

☐ The conclusion of this report is up front because most executives prefer to read it there — and because Maxwell Casio has no apparent reason to bury it in this report. ☐ Seldom will you have all the evidence to present a virtually airtight case. When you do, don't miss the opportunity. Casio didn't. He zeroed in on the evidence and did not present one extraneous detail.

SAMPLE C: MEMO REPORT

☐ Unlike Sample B, the conclusion in Sample C comes last because there is a reasonable chance that Ralph Morrow will not like Cliff Shoenfeld's counsel. By presenting the evidence first, Shoenfeld makes Morrow more receptive to the recommendation. ☐ Shoenfeld impartially presents and develops the evidence. He does not give the impression that he's out to torpedo John Murphy.

SAMPLE D: FORMAL PROPOSAL

☐ The title of the proposal spotlights dealer recruitment rather than trade-show participation. Peter Wong's primary concern is to recruit dealers. ☐ Throughout the proposal Wanda Fernandez anticipates and allays doubts that Wong might entertain. ☐ Fernandez uses a "kicker." Wong must act soon if he wants the good booth.

SAMPLE E: LETTER PROPOSAL

☐ Though this proposal is for a million-dollar contract, John Tantoni wrote a relatively short document because the issues are clear-cut and he and James Borg are on friendly terms. More words probably would have done more harm than good. ☐ Tantoni builds credibility by not sidestepping the fact that his competition delivers on shorter notice. Though he admits the fact, he does not apologize with a "Regrettably, . . ." or other repentant expression. He goes on to put his competition's advantage into perspective.

SAMPLE F: MEMO PROPOSAL

☐ Jean Tanaka identifies and rules out the other solutions to the parking space problem that might come to George Romanov's mind. ☐ Even if Romanov were to nix Tanaka's proposition, he probably would be impressed by how she researched and presented her proposal.

Bibliography

Academic and Entrepreneurial Research by Ilene N. Bernstein and Howard E. Freeman (Russell Sage Foundation, New York, 1975, 187 pages).

The Art of Winning Corporate Grants by Howard Hillman (Vanguard Press, New York, 1980, 180 pages).

The Art of Winning Foundation Grants by Howard Hillman and Karin Abarbanel (Vanguard Press, New York, 1975, 188 pages).

The Art of Winning Government Grants by Howard Hillman (Vanguard Press, New York, 1977, 246 pages).

The Art of Writing Effective Letters by Rosemary T. Fruehling and Sharon Bouchard (McGraw-Hill Book Company, New York, 1972, 257 pages).

Basic Grammar for Writing by Eugene Ehrlich and Daniel Murphy (McGraw-Hill Book Company, New York, 1971, 109 pages).

Better Business English by H. George Classen (Arco Publishing Company, New York, 1966, 108 pages).

Britannica Book of English Usage edited by Christine Timmons and Frank Girney (Doubleday & Company, Garden City, New York, 1980, 655 pages).

Business Communication: A Problem-Solving Approach, Second Edition by Roy W. Poe and Rosemary T. Fruehling (Gregg Division, McGraw-Hill Book Company, New York, 1978, 358 pages).

Business Communication Skills, A Career Focus by John J. Makay and Ronald C. Fetzer (D. Van Nostrand, New York, 1980, 352 pages).

The Business Communicator by Robert E. Swindle (Prentice-Hall, Englewood Cliffs, N.J., 1980, 368 pages).

Bibliography

Business English and Communication, Fifth Edition by Marie M. Steward, et al. (Gregg Division, McGraw-Hill Book Company, New York, 1978, 546 pages).

Business English for the 80's by Robert E. Barry (Prentice-Hall, Englewood Cliffs, N.J., 1980, 432 pages).

Business Research and Report Writing by Robert L. Shurter, et al. (McGraw-Hill Book Company, New York, 1965, 204 pages).

Business Writing by Jeanne Reed (Gregg Division, McGraw-Hill Book Company, New York, 1970, 160 pages).

The Careful Writer, A Modern Guide to English Usage by Theodore M. Bernstein (Atheneum, New York, 1979, 487 pages).

The Craft of Writing by Thomas Elliott Berry (McGraw-Hill Book Company, New York, 1974, 196 pages).

Developing Skills in Proposal Writing, Second Edition by Mary Hall (Continuing Education Publications, Portland, Ore., 1977, 339 pages).

The Dictionary of Do's and Don'ts, A Guide for Writers and Speakers by Harry G. Nickles (McGraw-Hill Book Company, 1974, 208 pages).

Effective Business Communications by Herta A. Murphy and Charles E. Peck (McGraw-Hill Book Company, New York, 1976, 703 pages).

Effective Research and Report Writing in Government by Jud Monroe (McGraw-Hill Book Company, New York, 1980, 320 pages).

Effective Writing by Robert Hamilton Moore (Rinehart & Company, New York, 1955, 588 pages).

The Elements of Style by Willard Strunk, Jr., revised by E.B. White (Macmillan Company, New York, 1979, 85 pages).

English Grammar and Structure by N. A. Berkoff (Arco Publishing Company, New York, 1963, 144 pages).

Bibliography

Executive's Guide to Effective Letters and Reports by William M. Parr (Parker Publishing Company, West Nyack, N.Y., 1976, 222 pages).

Good English with Ease by Samuel Beckoff (Arco Publishing Company, New York, 1976, 192 pages).

A Guide to Writing Research Papers by Dorothea M. Berry and Gordon P. Martin (McGraw-Hill Book Company, New York, 1971, 161 pages).

Harbrace College Handbook, Eighth Edition by John C. Hodges and Mary E. Whitten (Harcourt Brace Jovanovich, New York, 1977, 480 pages).

How to Lie with Statistics by Darrell Huff (W. W. Norton & Company, New York, 1954, 142 pages).

How to Prepare a Research Proposal, Second Edition by David R. Krathwohl (Syracuse University Bookstore, Syracuse, N.Y., 1977, 112 pages).

How to Write a Report Your Boss Will Read and Remember by Raymond V. Lesikar (Dow Jones-Irwin, Homewood, Ill., 1974, 216 pages).

How to Write Reports, Papers, Theses, Articles by John P. Riebel (Arco Publishing Company, New York, 1978, 121 pages).

The Macmillan Handbook of English, Third Edition by John M. Kierzek (The Macmillan Company, New York, 1954, 579 pages).

Make Yourself Clear by John O. Morris (McGraw-Hill Book Company, New York, 1972, 240 pages).

The Merriam-Webster Handbook of Effective Business Correspondence (Wallaby/Pocket Books, New York, 1979, 186 pages).

The Most Common Mistakes in English Usage by Thomas Elliott Berry (McGraw-Hill Book Company, New York, 1971, 146 pages).

Bibliography

Organization and Outlining by J. F. Pierce (Arco Publishing Company, New York, 1971, 144 pages).

The Proposal Writer's Swipe File II edited by Jean Brodsky (Taft Products, Washington, D.C., 1976, 136 pages).

Report Writing for Management by William J. Gallagher (Addison-Wesley Publishing Company, Reading, Mass., 1969, 216 pages).

The Rich Get Richer and the Poor Write Proposals by Nancy Mitiguy (University of Massachusetts, Amherst, Mass., 1978, 147 pages).

Style Guide by Janice L. Gorn (Simon and Schuster, New York, 1973, 107 pages).

Who-What-When-Where-How-Why-Made Easy by Mona McCormick (Quadrangle Books, Chicago, 1971, 192 pages).

The Writer's Resource Guide edited by William Brohaugh (Writer's Digest Books, Cincinnati, Ohio, 1979, 488 pages).

Writing About Science edited by Mary Elizabeth Bowen and Joseph A. Mazzeo (Oxford University Press, New York, 1979, 350 pages).

Writing: A Practical Guide for Business and Industry by Charles W. Ryan (John Wiley & Sons, New York, 1974, 256 pages).

Writing A Technical Paper by Donald H. Menzel, *et al.* (McGraw-Hill Book Company, New York, 1961, 132 pages).

Writing Communications in Business and Industry, Second Edition by Nelda R. Lawrence (Prentice-Hall, Englewood Cliffs, N.J., 1974, 167 pages).

Writing For Results In Business, Government, the Sciences and the Professions, 2nd Edition by David W. Ewing (John Wiley & Sons, New York, 1979, 456 pages).